Pakistan's Provinces

International Centre For Peace Initiatives

Strategic Foresight Group

Strategic Foresight Group

C-306 Montana, Lokhandwala Complex
Andheri West
Mumbai 400 053
India
E-mail: publications@peacein.com

Authors: Leena Pillai, Kumud-Pallavi Mutalik
Research Input: S Akbar Zaidi (Karachi), Mossarat Qadeem (Peshawar) with SFG research assistants
Creative Consultant: Sumedha Vaidya

ISBN 81-88262-05-6

Processed by Supressa Graphics Pvt Ltd and Printed at Pushpraj Printers, Mumbai.

Preface

Exactly two years ago, Strategic Foresight Group brought out a report, *The Future of Pakistan*. It has drawn considerable attention of policy makers in South Asia and beyond. It is the first time that a serious effort was made to map Pakistan's future trajectories.

The report, *Pakistan's Provinces*, is a continuation of the same effort. Our previous report had a macro level perspective. This report examines internal dynamics of each of the provinces and then assesses their collective impact. Normally, most studies observe a country in a top-bottom fashion. In Pakistan, considering the multitude of cultures that coexist, it is necessary to have a bottom-up approach.

With a bottom-up approach Pakistan looks like a bundle of four sticks tightly tied together in the middle with a string. In 1971, there were two big sticks and one fell apart under the heavy pressure of the string. In 2004, political discourse is increasingly including references to the 1971 situation. It doesn't mean that Pakistan's provinces will secede in 2004 or even in 2005. Yet, it remains to be seen whether they will be together until 2010.

The question of unity among provinces is linked to the broader issues of democracy and Pakistan's vision of its role in the region and the world. Despite the parliamentary elections of 2002 there is no doubt that democracy is a façade in the country. The appearance of democracy maybe adequate for Pakistan's friends abroad to justify support to its military regime. However internally democratic deficit has created vast space for religious, ethnic, and provincial separatist forces to operate. Obviously, the international community would not like to see Pakistan being disintegrated. But the examples of Iraq and Afghanistan prove that the international community has very little capacity to create unity in the face of internal divisions.

The objective of this report is to identify trends and discontinuities before it is too late to take corrective action. A stable and united Pakistan is in the interest of Pakistan's people, as well as its neighbours in South Asia. However, a stable and united Pakistan is only feasible when there is sincere democracy and a genuine commitment to regional peace. The unity of provinces is possible when the constituents have freedom from the pressure of a heavy rope. As the pressure is increasing, will the string hold together and for how long?

It is necessary to examine the above question in a dispassionate and analytical manner, based on hard facts. This is precisely what this report intends to do in the spirit of free intellectual inquiry. We invite the readers to use it constructively as the basis for a new debate that is long overdue.

SUNDEEP WASLEKAR
President
Strategic Foresight Group

Mumbai
June, 2004

Contents

Pakistan's 4-G Framework

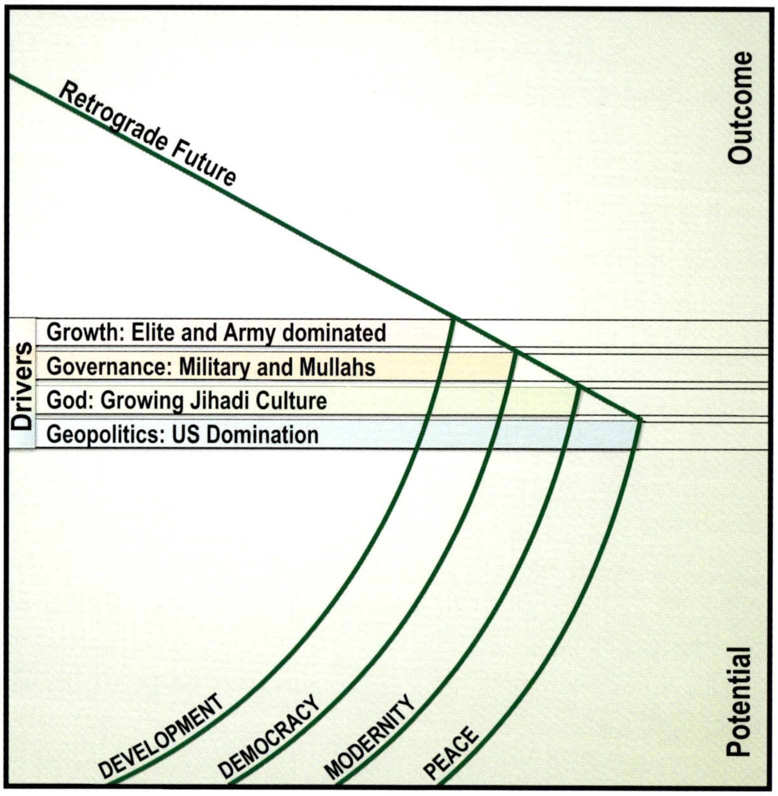

CHAPTER 1

Introduction

When General Pervez Musharraf, as he has indicated, divests his army uniform in December 2004, Pakistan will embark on a new trajectory.

Pakistan's future in the post-Musharraf era will not only have implications for Pakistan and India, but also for the United States. The new Pakistani army chief will be a person with strong personal links with the US, in fact who has lived in the US. While he can bank on personal goodwill, he might also be aware that signals from Washington are suggesting that policies are not a product of personal equations alone. In December 2004 he will accept General Musharraf as President, but by December 2005, General Musharraf will be irrelevant. Therefore, it is time to look beyond General Musharraf and deeper into Pakistan's dilemma in this decade.

Pakistan's biggest challenge will be in the context of relations between the federal government and the provinces. The last two years were marked by agitation in Sindh over the distribution of fiscal resources and water allocation. There have also been attacks on gas pipelines in Balochistan in a similar vein. The spring of 2004 saw the return of an exiled Balochi, Ataullah Mengal, who has revived the Pakistan Oppressed Nations Movement, challenging the centralized structure.

NWFP has evolved a new political system under the leadership of religious parties that is more akin to neighbouring Afghanistan of the 1990s than the progressive and moderate state that General Musharraf has envisioned. Even in Punjab, the largest province, there are signs of strife with the rise of a sub-national movement in the Seraiki region. It would be difficult for Pakistan to cope with these tendencies indefinitely, warranting the need for constructing democratic bridges between the federal government and provinces.

These processes will have implications for Pakistan's provinces. The democratization of institutions will enhance the role of political parties that are currently province-specific. For instance, the Muslim League is mainly a Punjab party, while People's Party is primarily influential in Sindh. The Muttahida Majlis-e-Amal (MMA) has following in NWFP and Balochistan.

The demand for re-organizing relations between the federal and provincial governments will have direct bearing on the future of provinces.

The recent increase in sub-nationalist tendencies can be partially attributed to the democratic deficit in the country. General Musharraf has weakened the two largest and powerful political parties, exiling their leaders. Religious parties and separatist groups are filling the vacuum thus created. If mainstream parties could function without encumbrance, religious and separatist parties would be obviated.

Pakistan's military ruler has a deal-making approach to politics. He seems to believe in resolving disputes between provinces through negotiations. Making structural changes in the political machinery seems nowhere on the agenda.

His strategy has facilitated the perpetuation of his own power, but has emaciated Pakistan's already weak democratic culture. The net outcome – rise in extremism, sectarianism and separatism.

In 1971, it was rejection of democracy that led to the division of Pakistan. If the army had honoured the electoral mandate, Sheikh Mujibur Rehman would have been Prime Minister and the country would have still been united. More than thirty years later, the army seems keen to undermine democracy and endanger the integrity of the nation. No wonder, references to 1971 are being made in the political rallies of 2004.

The future of Pakistan's provinces will have bearing on geo-politics of the entire region. Any tension between NWFP and the rest of Pakistan will impact Afghanistan. Problems in Balochistan will affect Afghanistan and Iran. Friction between Punjab and Sindh can cause, in the extreme case, massive refugee influx into India. Thus, the future of Pakistan's provinces will subtly govern the future of extended South Asia.

Attention to Pakistan's provinces is necessitated not only by tensions between Sindh and Punjab, but also by the fluidity in the region bordering Afghanistan and Pakistan. This fluidity always existed, it is the present uncertainty in Afghanistan that is making it significant.

Attention to Pakistan's provinces is also warranted by the increasing references being made to 1971-developments, in the country's political discourses. In 1971, Pakistan became the first major post-colonial state to bifurcate out of inter-provincial differences. In mid-1970s, it was again on the throes of fragmentation due to an agitation in Balochistan. Army intervention quelled the unrest and helped maintain the territorial integrity of residual Pakistan.

Every army chief has gifted Pakistan with loss of territory. General Yahya Khan lost East Pakistan, General Zia-ul-Haq lost Siachen, General Musharraf lost Afghanistan. The next chief runs the risk of losing a lot more, despite friends in a powerful land.

An analysis of Pakistan's provinces, at this juncture, is thus pertinent.

The study begins with a macro overview of Pakistan's economy followed by inter-provincial comparisons that are based on our understanding of Pakistan's economy and society. The subsequent chapters deal with each province separately. Finally, our perspectives are synthesized in an effort to outline future scenarios for Pakistan.

CHAPTER 2

Macroeconomic Overview

Pakistan's development process in the last five decades has been a series of transitions characterised by six different eras of economic policies and administrative choices. The first eleven years - 1947 to 1958 - marked the formative years of a new nation coming to terms with its rudiments whilst contending with the challenges of economy building. This was followed by what many term as the 'golden decade of economic development' under General Ayub Khan. Growth rates touched an unprecedented 6-7 per cent during this golden period, which concluded with the break-up of the country. Post-1971, Pakistan was a new state – less than half of the country it was in 1947.

The period of democracy under Zulfikar Ali Bhutto in the early 1970s was significant. It was a period of nationalisation of large parts of the economy and saw foundations of the capital goods industry being laid. His rule ended with the imposition of military rule under General Zia ul Haq in 1977. General Zia ruled for 11 years, during which the high-growth pattern re-emerged, promoted by large inflow of foreign aid, thanks to Pakistan's frontline role in the Afghanistan war. However, macroeconomic fundamentals were grossly slighted. General Zia's death saw the return of democracy in 1988, but with accompaniments – structural changes, economic liberalisation and privatisation. However, fiscal imbalances and poor governance vitiated economic growth during the 1990s. Between 1988 and 1997, four general elections saw as many new governments, with none completing the full term. Economic mismanagement and the absence of adequate external support slowed down economic growth considerably. In 1999, General Musharraf took over and re-imposed military rule. History repeated with Pakistan again chosen as a frontline state in the war against terror in 2001; foreign aid inflows revived.

The present economic strategy focuses entirely on restoring macroeconomic stability, reducing domestic and external debt, building foreign exchange reserves, acquiring aid and boosting investments. These policies have focused on stabilising the external economy. Internally, Pakistan is still afflicted by inadequate human and infrastructure development, as it struggles to strike equilibrium between democratic and military supremacy.

Economic Performance till the 1990s

The 1960s till the 1980s were the best years for Pakistan's economic development. Towards the end of the 1980s, a downturn set in that persisted through the 1990s.

Table 2.1: Average Annual Growth Rates

(Per cent)

	GDP	Agriculture	Manufacturing
1950s	3.1	1.6	-
1960s	6.8	5.1	9.9
1970s	4.8	2.4	5.5
1980s	6.5	5.4	8.2
1990s	4.6	4.4	4.8
1999-2002	3.3	1.6	4.5
2002-03	5.1	4.1	7.7

Source: Government of Pakistan, *Economic Survey 2002-03*, Islamabad, 2003, and State Bank of Pakistan, *Annual Report 2001-02*, Karachi, 2002. (The figures for 2002-03 are provisional figures).

A noteworthy factor in Pakistan's economic evolution is the direct relationship between foreign aid and economic growth. Stages of economic growth in Pakistan have always coincided with phases of enhanced foreign aid. The period of growth during the 1960s was dominated by the military rule of General Mohammad Ayub Khan, which saw the beginning of Pakistan's growing reliance on foreign aid. External economic assistance as per cent of GDP was a modest 2.8 per cent in 1960, but grew substantially to 6.6 per cent by 1965. In the 1980s too, under the military government of General Zia, Pakistan's economy grew on account of military and economic aid from the US and the West to counter the Soviet Union's designs in Afghanistan. Aid inflows reached $2 billion annually in the mid-1980s. Added to this, huge remittances from the Gulf States not only bolstered growth rates, but also impacted the social, economic and political structure of Pakistan.

In 1982-83, as much as $23.1 billion (equivalent to almost 10 per cent of GDP) was remitted to Pakistan. In 2003, Pakistan once again witnessed remittances peaking to $4 billion, replicating the days of past military rulers.

Pakistan has always treated external aid and remittances as an alternative to its internal resource generation. As a result, economic growth has merely been a surrogate of economic development, appearing when the foreign hand came forward and disappearing when the country was left to its own devices. Pakistan's excessive dependence on external sources has given it a trajectory of high growth, but at the cost of vitiated fundamentals of domestic economy.

Poor Human Development

Pakistan has witnessed an uneven relationship between GDP growth and poverty. The country experienced GDP stagnation and poverty in the 1950s, increasing poverty despite good GDP growth in the 1960s, declining poverty along with stagnation in GDP growth in the 1970s, declining poverty and expanding GDP growth in the 1980s and finally, increasing poverty and decreasing GDP growth in the 1990s.

Today there are at least 47 million people below the poverty line. Poverty first rose in the 1960s, after which it has seen a continuous decline until around 1987-88, after which, there has been another rise in poverty incidence.

In the 1980s, high remittance was primarily responsible for the fall in poverty. Income per capita during the period rose by 3.2 per cent a year, compared to the 3.9 per cent rise recorded in the 1960s. Development expenditure continued to be high for most of the 1980s, as did spending on social sectors. Poverty levels dropped. The trend of increasing public sector employment began in the 1970s and continued into the decade of the eighties; urban and rural wages also showed an increase. In a way, the most important contributor to growth and to poverty alleviation during this period was remittances from the Middle East.

The scenario changed considerably after 1988. The 1990s witnessed a 7 per cent annual increase in poverty, with poverty incidence reaching 31 per cent in 2001.The poverty pool expanded from 24 million in 1990-91 to about 47 million in 2003.

Several factors contributed to the sudden increase in poverty levels during the 1990s. Firstly, the overall growth rate of

GDP stooped well below trend levels, and appreciably below the average of the 1980s. In 1992-93 and in 1996-97, GDP growth was 2.27 per cent and 1.3 per cent, respectively, the lowest in over three decades. Since 1988, inflation has been in double digits in seven years, while in the preceding 40 years (1947-87), inflation was in double digits on only seven occasions. Moreover, the growth rate of real per capita income in the period 1991-98 was only 1.3 per cent – inadequate to make any significant alleviation in poverty. Additionally, remittances, which had played such an important role in the 1970s and 1980s in alleviating poverty, declined by about 41.8 per cent (in constant prices) between 1982-83 and 1995-96, and in 1998-99, they were the lowest since 1978-79.

Table 2.2: Poverty in Pakistan

(% to total population)

Year	Total	Rural	Urban
1963-64	40.2	38.9	44.5
1969-70	46.5	49.1	38.8
1979	30.7	32.5	25.9
1984-85	24.5	25.9	21.2
1987-88	17.3	18.3	15.0
1992-93	22.4	23.3	15.5
1998-99	30.6	34.7	20.9
2003	31.8	38.6	22.4

Source: Government of Pakistan, *Pakistan Economic Survey*, various issues, Islamabad.

Weak Industrial Sector

At one stage, the manufacturing sector with growth rates averaging 9.1 per cent between 1980-88 played a stellar role in Pakistan's economic growth. This rate fell to an average of 4.9 per cent for the period 1988-97, and further to -0.1 per cent in 1996-97 (lowest in the last thirty years), to reach 1.5 per cent in 1999-2000. As a rather selfish means of containing fiscal deficits, Pakistan has been cutting public expenditure, and more alarmingly, development expenditure. From a high of 9.3 per cent of GDP in 1980-81, development expenditure has been gradually declining. Since 1997-98, it has been only a little over three per cent of GDP.

Pakistan has a narrow industrial base, with some resource-based industries and few engineering branches. Pakistan has had modest development in steel, textiles, sugar, cement, leather goods, chemicals plastics and few other industries. However, the industrial sector rests precariously on agro-based industries, which account for 49 per cent of value added in the manufacturing sector. Export earnings are largely dominated by textiles an agro-based sector.

Ineffective policies and neglect is responsible for Pakistan's weak industrialisation. The prime factor, however, is the uncertain political and security environment, which inhibits huge capital investment. Most industrial development in Pakistan is in agro-based industries or consumer goods. The industrial sector growth is in direct relation to an agro-services-led-progress and is primarily influenced by textiles. Remittances have improved the demand for consumer durables.

Precarious Agriculture and Water Situation

Since the late 1990s, growth in agriculture has distinctly slowed down. The annual growth registered between 1996-2001 was a mere two per cent. Fiscal 2000-01 and 2001-02 was the worst with the agriculture sector suffering a decline of 2.7 per cent and 0.1 per cent respectively. However, fiscal 2002-03 picked up registering a growth of 4.1 per cent, due to increased water availability.

Two core weaknesses impinge upon Pakistan's agriculture:

- Structural limitations such as low productivity and skewed land-owning patterns
- Declining water availability

Agricultural growth in the past was primarily achieved through an increase in area under cultivation, rather than enhancement in productivity. The strategy of increasing farm output through the expansion of land has strangulated yield-enhancement efforts. Today, as Pakistan reaches its physical limits in terms of expansion of agricultural land, only intensive farming and land reforms can arrest falling productivity levels. Intensive farming can be achieved by diverting resources to enable technological coverage. The other factor – land reforms – can be possible only if there is a structural transformation in the political and social landscape.

Severe drought conditions have been plaguing the agriculture sector since 1996, which has resulted in damages to the tune of over $2 billion - the worst period being from years 2000 to 2002. With agriculture consuming 90 per cent of the fresh water available, irrigation is critical to the economic development of Pakistan. Irrigation sustains agricultural production that provides food security and generates employment and export earnings.

Irrigated land accounts for over 80 per cent of cropland and irrigated agriculture contributes over 90 per cent to the farm produce. Pakistan has the highest irrigated to rainfed land ratio of 4:1 in the world. It also has the world's largest contiguous irrigation network. The country is entirely dependent on natural river flows to feed this vast network and hence water management and its distribution are core issues of concern.

However, Pakistan is rapidly turning into a water-scarce country. Per capita water availability has drastically declined to 1,200 cubic metres in 2003 from about 5,600 cubic metres in 1947 - at an abatement rate of about 2.7 per cent per annum. Water availability is estimated to fall further to the threshold level of 1,000 cubic metres by 2010, assuming the total population then touches 170 million, growing at 2.1 per cent per year. Water availability for irrigation also is diminishing. From an average canal inflow of 136.9 million acre feet (MAF) during 1980-1997, the flow had declined by 33 per cent to 91.15 MAF in 2001-02. Fiscal 2002-03, a year of above-normal rainfall still witnessed an 18 per cent shortfall in irrigation water supply.

Major problems afflicting the sustainability of water and land resources of Pakistan are:

- Near-maximum exploitation of existing storage capacity
- Sedimentation of reservoirs leading to reduced storage capacities
- Weak irrigation system leading to a concurrent situation of floods and drought The sudden release of water, after a prolonged dry spell, has resulted in major cracks in canals, particularly in arid Sindh
- Loss of land due to salinity and waterlogging
- Sea intrusion in the Indus delta.

With a growing population and declining water availability, food security can prove a major issue in Pakistan in days to come, unless it revamps its irrigation system on a war footing and develops new water-storage facilities.

Table 2.3: External Debt in the 1990s

($ billion)

	Total Debt Outstanding			Annual Debt Servicing		
	Long Term	Short/Mid Term	Total	Principal	Interest	Total
1990-91	15.471	1.824	17.295	1.669	0.711	2.381
1991-92	17.361	2.268	19.629	2.086	0.767	2.853
1992-93	19.044	3.002	22.046	2.130	0.814	2.944
1993-94	20.322	4.160	24.483	2.722	0.890	3.612
1994-95	22.117	4.409	26.526	3.304	1.020	4.324
1995-96	22.275	5.460	27.735	3.262	1.085	4.347
1996-97	23.145	5.140	28.285	4.038	1.042	5.080
1997-98	23.042	5.940	28.982	3.575	1.095	4.670
1998-99	23.101	6.572	29.673	1.905	0.752	2.657
1999-2000	23.834	5.622	32.746*	2.366	1.377	3.743

* Includes the 'New Category' of debt worth $ 3.29, introduced by the State Bank of Pakistan that year, which had not been included in previous formats.
Source: State Bank of Pakistan, *Annual Report*, Various Years, Karachi.

Heavy External Debt

Pakistan's total debt had touched a preposterous 100 per cent of GDP in mid-2001. The country was dogged by large fiscal deficits, at the average rate of 7 per cent of GDP, for two decades beginning from the 1980s. The associated build-up of public debt led to serious fiscal imbalances.

Public debt grew at an average rate of almost 16 per cent per annum during the 1980s and 1990s. Steady depreciation in the Pakistani rupee and the high cost of borrowings were also responsible for accumulation of public debt.

Perhaps the most astonishing factor is that net addition to total debt outstanding in the period 1990-2000 was $15.451 billion while in the same period the total amount repaid as interest and principal was $36.611 billion. Pakistan had been making average repayments to its loans enacted over many decades of the order of $3.66 billion annually in the 1990s, and yet, had seen its external liabilities almost double. Much of these repayments had been based upon increased borrowing, suggesting that a substantial proportion of new loans were not deployed for national development but was used instead to retire old debt.

Major factors leading to the rapid accumulation of external debt include:

- Persistently large current account deficit
- Imprudent use of borrowed resources, such as wasteful government spending and borrowing for non-development expenditure
- Weakening of debt-servicing capacity in terms of stagnant foreign exchange earnings and rising cost of external borrowing.

Pakistan was categorised as a highly debted nation and was on the verge of defaulting in its payments. However, the Afghan war in 2001 redeemed Pakistan as it could hope to see external funding and aid flows reviving. Pakistan's time-honoured growth model of seeking prosperity through borrowings and other external sources perpetuated.

Economic Growth: A Surrogate of Foreign Aid

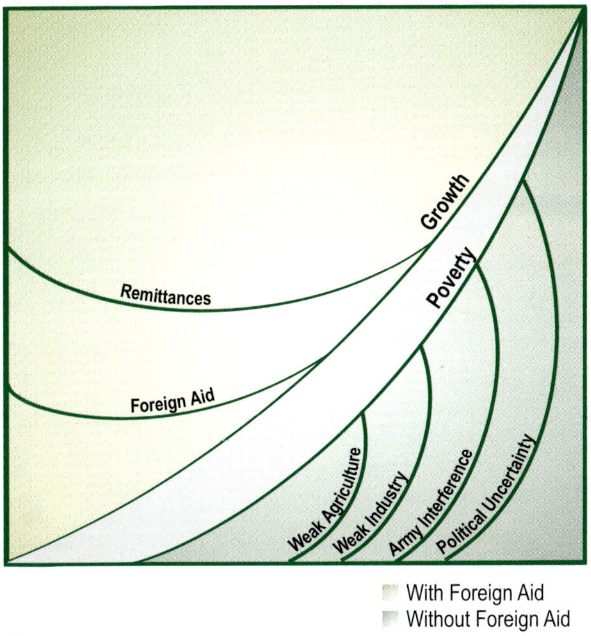

Black Economy

As a dubious consequence of a weak state apparatus and an execrable performance by the formal sector, black money and the informal sector are keeping Pakistan's economy afloat.

According to the Pakistan Institute of Development Economics, assets worth more than $28 billion are stashed away in the underground or black economy. World Bank has estimated black economy at around 70 per cent of GDP in 2001.

Since October 2001, the government has been gaining some control on a specific segment of the black economy – the *hawala* market, or the illegal trade in foreign currencies. Traditionally, overseas Pakistanis have been repatriating funds through illegal channels known as *hawala*. With the crackdown on illegal transactions in the international banking system, as a part of the worldwide war on terror, *hawala* channels have almost frozen. As a result, overseas Pakistanis have to remit funds through official channels, thus increasing remittances to three times in the last months of 2001 as compared to the last months of 2000. As a consequence, Pakistan's foreign exchange reserves improved to almost $12 billion in April 2004 and the rupee strengthened from Rs.64 per US$ in October 2001 to Rs.57 in April 2004.

Black economy has devastating social and political effects. For one, it promotes the underworld, as smuggling, tax evasion and *hawala* transactions require criminal expertise. Pakistan's dependence on the black economy for economic survival reflects a distorted value system. It creates a criminalized society and a conflict-oriented state with vested interest in protecting smugglers, illicit arms traders, terrorists and religious fundamentalists. These elements, in turn, undermine the formal economy.

Agriculture, the Driving Force

The strong correlation between politics and economics has been responsible for the agriculture-intensive development of Pakistan. At attaining sovereignty, Pakistan had a small number of powerful landowners with large land holdings and a domineering effect over the polity. In the early 1950s, 7 per cent of landowners occupied over 50 per cent of the agricultural acreage. Majority of the population consisted of tenant farmers who cultivated small plots. With almost no industry, Pakistan mainly produced agricultural raw material that was supplied to processing companies in India.

The precarious nature of Pakistan's economic base – vast natural resources but extreme industrial backwardness – was soon transformed with adequate emphasis on building an industrial base. Pakistan managed to achieve rapid economic expansion, which substantially altered the structure of the economy:

- Agriculture's share declined from 53 per cent of GDP in 1950 to 25 per cent in 2003
- Share of industry rose from 8 per cent of GDP in 1950 to 21 per cent in 2003
- The services sector grew extensively, especially in the 1980s and 1990s, and now accounts for over 50 per cent of GDP
- From an industrial base of 11 large-scale units in 1947, Pakistan in 2000 had over 2700 such units.

Table 2.4: Leadership of Political Parties in Pakistan in 2001

Name of Party	Party Head	Background
PML (Quaid-e-Azam)	Shujaat Hussain	Industrialist
Pakistan People's Party	Benazir Bhutto	Landlord
PML (N)	Nawaz Sharief	Industrialist
PML (Functional)	Pir Sahib Paghara	Landlord
PML (Junejo)	Hamid Nasir Chatta	Landlord
Awami National Party	Asfandyar Wali Khan	Landlord
Pakistan Democratic Party	Nawabzada Nasrullah Khan	Landlord
Millat Party	Farooq Leghari	Ex-Civil Servant
NPP	Ghulam Mustafa Jatoi	Landlord
PAP	Fanoor Gojar	Agriculturist
Sindh Nationalist Front	Mumtaz Ali Bhutto	Landlord
Sindh Democratic Alliance	Imtiaz Sheikh	Ex-Civil Servant
Jamhoori Watan Party	Akbar Khan Bugti	Landlord
Balochistan Nationalist Party	Akhtar Mengal	Landlord
Jamaat-e-Islami	Qazi Hussain Ahmad	Religious Jurist
JUI (S)	Maulana Nimatullah	Religious Teacher
JUI (F)	Maulana Fazlur Rehman	Religious Teacher

Source: *Struggling for Survival: State of Political Parties in Pakistan* by Zafarullah Khan

Table 2.5: Military Persons in Key Economic Institutions

Karachi Electric Supply Co. (Chairman)	:	Lt. General Zulfikar Ali Khan
Karachi Elect. Supply Co. (MD)	:	Brig. Tariq Mehmood Khan Sadozai
Lahore Electric Supply Co. (CEO)	:	Brig. Riaz Ahmad Toor
Peshawar Electric Supply Co. (CEO)	:	Brig. Tahir Saeed Malik
Islamabad Electric Supply Co. (CEO)	:	Brig. Waseem Zafar Iqbal
Hyderabad Electric Supply Co. (CEO)	:	Brig. (retd) Muhammad Tariq Arshad
Quetta Electric Supply Co.(CEO)	:	Brig. Tasadduq Hussain Shah
Oil & Gas Regulatory Authority (Secretary)	:	Brig. (retd.) Tariq Mehmood
Oil & Gas Devp Co. (Managing Dir.)	:	Major General Pervez Akmal
Pakistan Telecommunication Authority (Chairman)	:	Lt. Gen (retd) Abdul Qayyum
Karachi Port Trust (Chairman)	:	Rear Admiral Ahmed Hayat
Gwadar Port Authority (Chairman)	:	Rear Admiral (retd) Sarfraz Khan
Port Bin Qasim Authority (Chairman)	:	Rear Admiral Sikandar V Naqvi
National Highway Authority (Chairman)	:	Maj. Gen. Farukh Javed
Export Promotion Bureau (Chairman)	:	Capt (retd.) Naveed Akram Cheema
Pakistan Tourism Devp Corp. (MD)	:	Maj Gen. Anis Ahmad Bajwa
Pakistan National Shipping Corp (Chairman)	:	Vice Admiral (retd) S Tauqeer Naqvi
Civil Aviation Authority (Chairman)	:	Air Marshall (retd) Salim Arshad
(Director)	:	Air Cdre. (retd) Shahid Naveed
Pakistan Post Office (Dir. General)	:	Maj Gen (retd.) Agha Masood Hassan
Pakistan Intl. Airlines Investments (Chairman)	:	Lt. Gen. (retd) Hamid Nawaz Khan

Source: Compiled from various Pakistani Newspapers. Appointments as of January 2004.

However, despite these modest strides in development, the country retained its agrarian characteristics - its heavy dependence on agriculture for sustenance subsists. Though the contribution of agriculture to GDP has come down to 25 per cent over the years, the share of agro-based industries increased to a substantial 50 per cent of value added in the manufacturing sector. Also, 70 per cent of the population is either directly or indirectly dependent on the agriculture sector for its livelihood. Agriculture accounts for 70 per cent of Pakistan's export earnings. As a result, even today, agriculture exerts an important influence on Pakistan's overall growth.

Agriculture has also galvanised landlords into a powerful political force. Since Independence, two land reforms have been implemented, but land owning patterns have largely remained unaltered. There are 5.1 million farms in the country, of which 93 per cent are small farms (up to 10 hectares). Large farms, though only 7 per cent of the total, account for 40 per cent of the total cultivated area.

The failure of land reforms is not surprising. Landlords have dominated political institutions and many of them have been heads of government - both federal and provincial. Further, alliances with the military and the bureaucracy have given the land-owning families added clout. Beginning with the present Prime Minister of Pakistan, Mir Zafarullah Khan Jamali, who is a landlord from Balochistan, several other national-level political parties are headed by landlords, industrialists, or ex-bureaucrats. In the 2002 elections, 25 parties had their heads elected to the national assembly of which 11 were either landlords or had association with the agriculture sector.

The flagrant promotion of a certain class of people has led to nation-wide inequalities in income distribution, human development as well as regional development. Many of Pakistan's grave political, economic and social problems, including the failure of parliamentary democracy to take roots, emanate from its unitary, highly centralised, and authoritarian structure of the state and the forces that sustain it.

Military's Corporate Ventures

Another powerful component in Pakistan's power structure is the military. Pakistani military's business activities revolve around four major foundations: *Fauji* Foundation (FF), Army Welfare Trust (AWT), *Shaheen* Foundation (SF) and *Bahria* Foundation. These four major welfare foundations operate a number of corporate ventures with interests ranging from the sugar, cereal and fertilizer production, aviation, real estate, education and advertising. These assets run into millions of dollars but with little accountability.

The largest by far, is the Fauji Foundation, with declared assets amounting to Rs.9.8 billion in 2003 with a total of 11 major projects out of which six are shareholding projects.

Aggrandizing its Fauji Foundation-led domination, the Army established another foundation: the Army Welfare Trust. Although the Trust became fully operational in 1977, it was originally registered as a 'society' in 1971 under the Societies Registration Act of 1860 with an endowment of Rs.0.7 million. The trust, runs 26 independent projects, valued at Rs.17 billion.

The Army's General Head Quarters fully manages these organizations. The chief of the service is the head of the governing board that includes all the senior staff officers of the Army Chief. The division of business under the two heads – AWT and Askari – is linked with privatization. Projects having majority private equity fall under Askari management.

The other two defence forces disapproved the complete domination of corporate activities by the Army. The Pakistan Air Force was the first to respond by establishing the *Shaheen* Foundation in 1977 under the Charitable Endowments Act, 1889. The foundation had an initial investment of Rs.5 million, donated equally by the PAF and the federal government. Today, the Foundation claims to have an annual turnover of Rs.600 million. Reportedly, 10-20 per cent of the annual profits is spent on welfare activities.

The Navy was the last to start its own welfare foundation. It did so in 1981 with an initial grant of Rs.3 million from the Pakistan Navy's own welfare funds. Unlike the other foundations, *Bahria's* ventures are fairly small and rely mostly on private investment. The foundation at present has 19 projects.

Apart from its involvement in corporate activities, the military also holds several key positions in economic institutions. In General Musharraf's journey from the CEO of the country to the President, over 1000 retired military generals were appointed to important civilian institutions. Most economic institutions, especially in the infrastructure sector, are run by persons having military background. These appointments have indirectly helped military-supported corporate entities.

The military of Pakistan has pervaded every segment – industry, commerce, diplomatic services and civil institutions. The four foundations represent the biggest business conglomerate in the country. Even private corporate companies find it difficult to compete with these military organisations as the latter enjoy several tax exemptions, subsidised electricity, strong political connections and virtual freedom from accountability. Their stakes in Pakistan's economy are high.

Pakistan's Elite Economy

The first quarter century of Pakistan's existence was an uninterrupted process of concentration of power, where both economic and political power was held by a small coterie of elites. This resulted in skewed allocation of resources.

As a result, income disparities are very prominent in Pakistan. The average income of people in the highest population quintile in Pakistan is over seven times higher than that of the lowest. This phenomenon is the same for both urban and rural areas. However, this is only a crude reflection of income disparities in Pakistan.

The World Bank, in its study on income disparities in Pakistan, has revealed that in 1998-99, the top 20 per cent of the

Military's Corporate Ventures

Army Welfare

- Askari Stud Farms
- Askari Farms
- Askari Welfare Rice Mill
- Askari Welfare Sugar Mill
- Askari Fish Farm
- Askari Cement
- Askari Welfare Pharmaceutical Project
- Magnesite Refineries
- Army Welfare Shoe Project
- Army Welfare Woolen Mill
- Army Welfare Hosiery Unit
- AWT Commercial Plazas
- Army Welfare Shops
- Army Welfare Commercial Project
- Askari Commercial Bank
- Askari Leasing Limited
- Askari General Insurance Company
- Askari Welfare Saving Scheme
- Askari Associate Limited
- Askari Information Service
- Askari Guards Limited
- Askari Power Limited
- Askari Commercial Enterprises
- Askari Aviation
- Askari Housing Scheme (At six different locations)
- Three travel agencies.

Bahria Foundation

- Falah Trading Agency
- Bahria Construction
- Bahria Travel and Recruiting Agency
- Bahria Paints
- Bahria Deep Sea Fishing
- Bahria Complexes
- Bahria Town and Housing Schemes
- Bahria Dredging
- Bahria Ship Breaking
- Bahria Diving and Salvage International
- Bahria University
- Bahria Shipping
- Bahria Coastal Services
- Bahria Security & System Services
- Bahria Catering and Decoration Services
- Bahria Farming
- Bahria Holdings
- Bahria Harbor Services
- Bahria Bakery

Fauji Foundation

- Fauji Sugar Mills
- Fauji Cereal
- Fauji Corn Complex
- FONGAS (Natural gas supply company)
- Fauji Poly Propylene Products
- Fauji Fertilizer Company (FFC)
- Fauji Jordan Company (FJFC)
- Mari Gas Company
- Fauji Cement
- Fauji Oil Terminal Company Project (FOTCO)
- Fauji Kabirwala Power Company (under construction).

Shaheen Foundation

- Shaheen Air International
- Shaheen Air Cargo
- Shaheen Airport Services
- Shaheen Aerotraders
- Shaheen Insurance
- Shaheen Complex
- Shaheen Pay TV
- FM-100 (Radio channel)
- Shaheen System (Information Technology)
- Shaheen Knitwear

population accounted for 42.3 per cent of the income and consumption expenditure. The Gini coefficient for Pakistan at 0.4 reflects moderate disparity in income levels.

Strategic Foresight Group has assessed the economy on the basis of consumption patterns. As of 2002-2003, there were around 3 million Internet users, 2.6 million mobile phone subscribers, 0.7 million cars and 0.6 million personal computers. About 1.5 million people travel by air. Pakistan has about 19.2 million households accommodating 140 million people. Evidently, there are 5 lakh households that enjoy these facilties, comprising of 2.5 million people

Table 2.6: Average Per Capita Income by Income Quintile, 1996-97

(Rs. per month)

Income Quintile	Urban	Rural	Overall
First	482	338	360
Second	692	490	538
Third	912	641	713
Fourth	1,286	870	981
Fifth	2,972	2,268	2,530

Source: Estimates based on HIES (1996-97).

considering an average size of 5 persons per household. In other words, about 1.6 per cent of Pakistan's population enjoy the luxuries of life. They read English newspapers, have personal computers, have access to the Internet, travel abroad. This segment can be termed as the ruling class, comprising of landlords having large land holdings, industrialists, bureaucrats and military generals.

The segment leading a peripheral life comprises 98.5 per cent of the population. This segment can be further subdivided into people living a lower middle class life and those below the poverty levels.

About 13 million households live above poverty levels, but lead a meagre lifestyle. There are hardly 2.2 million television sets, 2.3 million two-wheelers, 3.7 million telephone connections. This implies that hardly 2 million households in this segment have amenities like telephones, two-wheelers and television sets. Most of them have electricity connections, but only 5.5 million households receive tap water and 3.5 million have LPG gas connections. Thus, less than 50 per cent of the households in this segment enjoy even basic amenities of life. Most of them live in abject privation. This segment accommodates a population of about 91 million, based on an average per household size of 7 persons.

Another 5.7 million households, comprising 45 million people, live below poverty levels.

Post 2000: Impact of 9/11

An extraordinary turnaround took place in Pakistan's fortunes and macroeconomic status since 9/11. As the financial year 2002-03 drew to a close, all macroeconomic indicators looked revitalised and the government announced that the economy was in its 'take-off' stage. Economy was reviving and so was investor interest.

The turnaround post 9/11 provided Pakistan with acutely needed fiscal space. The attacks of September 11, 2001, in New York, and the US war in Afghanistan brought Pakistan back into 'frontline' status, similar to the 1980s whilst fighting another Afghan war. The positive outcome of 9/11 were:

- Foreign exchange reserves rose above $12.6 billion by end of fiscal 2003-04, up from a mere $ 1 billion in 1999.
- Exports grew by 20 per cent crossing $11 billion for the first time ever, as quota restrictions on Pakistani textiles were waived by the US and the European Union.
- The most significant development has been the increase in home remittances, which have grown 300 per cent since 11 September 2001. Remittances into Pakistan increased to an amazing $4 billion, the highest ever, equivalent to more than 5 per cent of GDP.
- Inflation was brought down to around 4 per cent, the rupee appreciated by six per cent in the last three years and there was a current account surplus.
- Debt-scheduling agreement between Paris Club donors and Pakistan worth $12.5 billion, which was nearly one-third the total external debt of the country in 2001, reducing annual debt servicing and the annual debt liability. An estimated relief of $1.2 billion to $1.5 billion would accrue annually in interest payments on external debt in the medium term, up to 2004-05. Given Pakistan's earlier debt profile, this is an important development, which takes pressure of government finances and allows a huge amount of fiscal breathing space.
- Pakistan managed to retire some of its expensive debt to multilateral agencies. In January 2004, Pakistan remitted $1.17 billion to the Asian Development Bank and retired one of its most expensive debts.
- Numerous sanctions related to Pakistan's nuclear tests and military coup were set aside.

Pakistan's Economic Standards

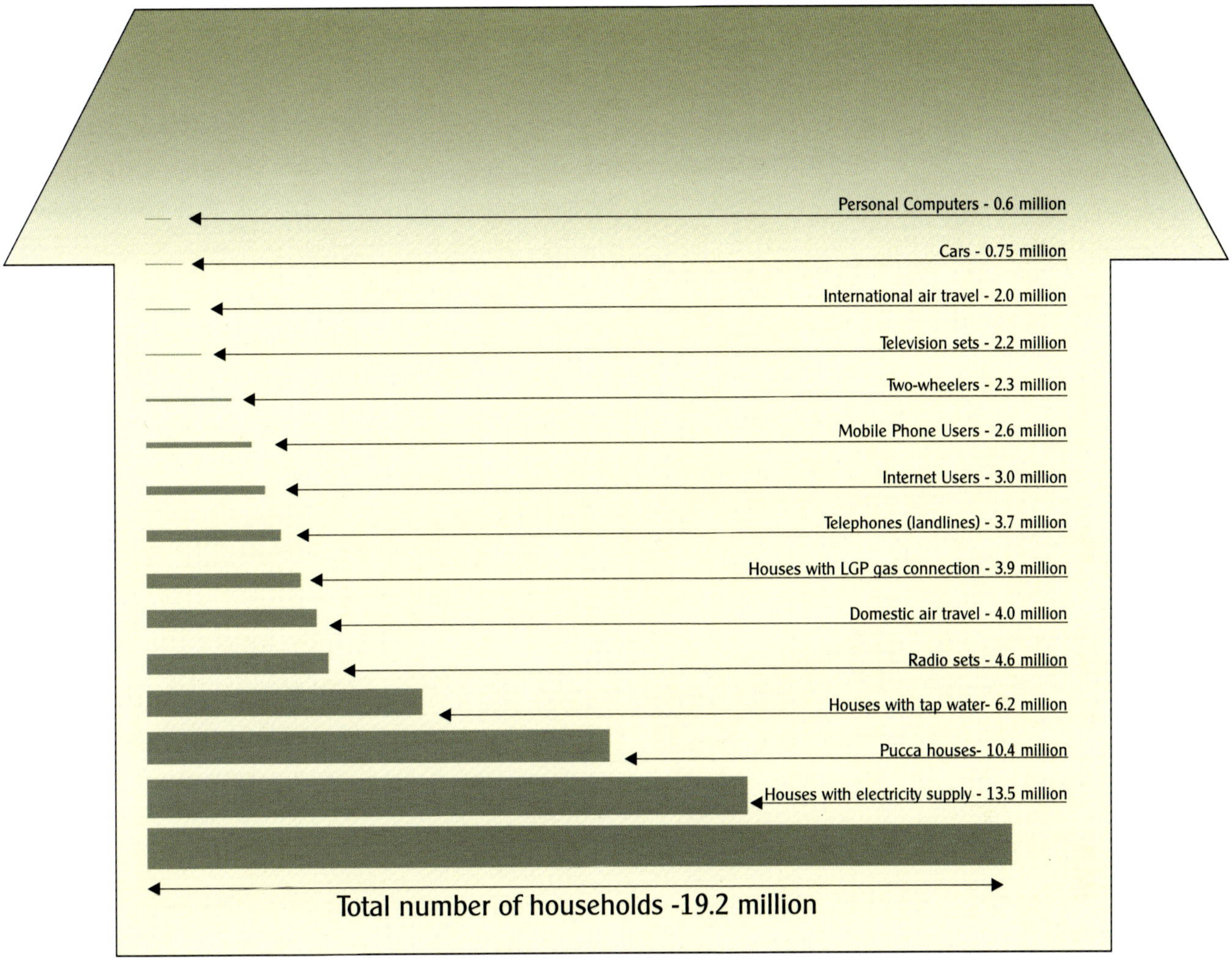

- There was considerable Increase in foreign direct investment and the Karachi Stock Exchange crossed the psychological 4,000 index mark for the first time ever.
- Coincidentally, the agriculture sector also improved its performance on account of improved rains and water availability during the year.
- As a final culmination, the growth for fiscal 2002-03 increased to 5.1 per cent – the highest annual real growth rate since 1995-96.

Pakistan's reversal of fortunes was led by fortuitous international political factors, rather than improved economic policies or better fiscal management.

Foreign-aid/remittances Subsidised Economy

Post 9/11, Pakistan witnessed an upsurge in home remittances with fiscal 2002-03 recording a historical high of $4.23 billion. Another contributing factor was large cash transfers made by the US to Pakistan for the latter's support to the US in its war against terrorism. Such transfers amounted to over $2 billion during 2001-2003. This includes two grants of $50 million each immediately after declaration of support, followed by a further cash grant of $600 million in early 2002 and $1.2 billion worth of reimbursements till March 2003 for Pakistan's logistics support.

Summary of Pakistan's Economy in 2000-01

- GDP growth – 2 %
- Total debt - 105 % of GDP
- Savings rate - 12-14 % of GDP
- Development expenditure - 3.2 % of GDP
- Poverty incidence - 35 %
- Agriculture sector - -2.7 %
- Drought damage – upwards of $2 billion.

The improved inflow of remittances could be ascribed to the following reasons:

- In 2002, the crackdown on *hawala* network led to a collapse of the kerb market premium and consequently proved a turnaround in the exchange rate management strategy. In 1998, when the *Hundi* system flourished, there was a difference of almost Rs.10 between the bank rates and the open market rates of the dollar. However, following the crackdown, people now prefer to remit through official banking channels.
- The freezing of foreign currency deposits in May 1998, following the nuclear test sanctions imposed on Pakistan, had eroded the confidence of overseas Pakistanis. Since 2002, Pakistan has followed a policy of liberalising the foreign exchange market. Added to this, the appreciation of the rupee has helped bring back Pakistani deposits held abroad. Also, migrants were allowed to hold forex accounts within the country.
- The banking sector in the United States and European countries started scrutinising deposits of immigrants in the wake of events of 9/11. This factor increased remittance flows from these countries, especially the US. Perhaps this is also why the highest remittances in 2002-03 came from the US and not from any single country in the Middle East, as was the case in the 1980s.
- Remittances from UAE are the second highest. With a view to tap this source, in 2001, Pakistan government announced special incentives like reduction in transaction costs, concession in rate of interest on loans taken from banks, for Pakistanis living in the UAE for home remittances through legal channels. This gave a major impetus to cash inflows from UAE

Of all the above-mentioned factors, the crackdown on *hawala* system proved most effective in augmenting home remittances. Estimates suggest that Pakistanis have at least $32 billion in foreign banks.

However, first half of fiscal 2003-04, saw a marked decline in inflow of remittances, especially from the US and UAE. Remittances from UAE fell by 44 per cent during the period July-October 2003, while those from the US declined by 16 per cent. These two countries combined account for almost half of the total remittances received. The reasons cited for the decline are:

- US authorities had started questioning all money transfers of $5,000 or more directed towards Pakistan
- UAE was more stringent on conditions to disclose the whereabouts of the money transfers worth Rs.1.6 lakh or more
- In the bargain, *hundiwalas* partly recaptured their lost market share.

Buoyed Economy: Partly a Statistical Gimmick

During 2001-02, Pakistan undertook a major exercise in titivating its statistical data. Definitions were modified, drastic retrospective revisions were made, sampling techniques were changed or partial data was presented. This in a way, made Pakistan's economic indicators appear revitalised, albeit insubstantially.

In 1999-2000, the Economic Survey projected poverty incidence at 33.5 per cent of population for 2000-01. As per estimates presented by the Mahbub-ul-Haq Human Development Centre, poverty incidence had touched 35 per cent of total population by end of 2001. However, the Economic Survey of 2002-03 presented a revised version of

Richness through Redenifition

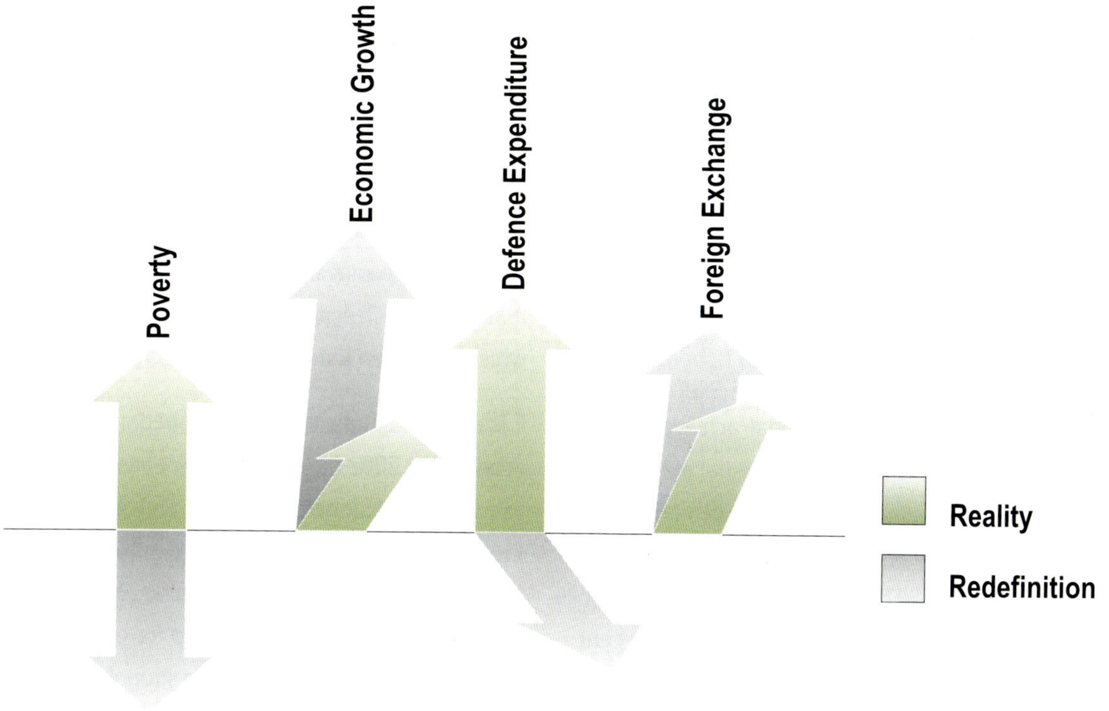

poverty estimates, showing poverty levels to have touched 32 per cent in 2000-01, which remained almost constant in 2003.

Through a notification issued on April 8, 2001, poverty was redefined based on intake of 2,350 calories per day, as against the previous level of 2,150 calories per day. This revision inflated poverty levels drastically. Hitherto believed period of lowest poverty levels in 1987-88 at 17 per cent was revised to 29 per cent under the new definition. For 1990-91, data was revised from 22 per cent to 26 per cent. However, for 1996-97, the poverty incidence intriguingly reduced from 31 per cent to 29.8 per cent!

Since 1998-99, poverty trends have sort of been arrested according to the revised definition. Between 1998-99 and 2001-02, the economy has grown by hardly 2.8 per cent per year, while poverty has shown an increase of only two percentage points.

The methodology for calculating foreign exchange reserves also underwent a change in fiscal 2000-01. According to the new definition, foreign exchange reserves would include in addition to free reserves with State Bank of Pakistan, reserves with ADs (FE-25 deposits). According to the new definition, Pakistan's foreign exchange reserves rose to $3,219 million as on June 2001 from $1,968 million on June 2000. On the basis of the previous definition, liquid reserves increased from $991 million in June 2000 to $1,677 million on June 2001. Nevertheless, there has been a real steady increase in the foreign exchange reserves of Pakistan, not merely reflecting a change in accounting techniques.

Since fiscal 2000-01, defence expenditure is being calculated net of defence pensions. As a result, defence expenditure in 2000-01 showed a sudden decline of 12.8 per cent, to subsequently increase by 13.6 per cent in 2001-02 and further by 6 per cent in 2002-03. Also, as per cent of total

Table 3.3: Per Capita Provincial GDP at Constant Factor Cost (1980-81 prices)

(in Rupees)

	Punjab	Sindh	NWFP	Balochistan
1981	2972	4431	2803	2397
1990	3849	NA	3355	3081
1999	4619	6090	4662	3775
Annual growth in income (% change 1999 over 1981)				
	2.5	1.8	2.9	2.5

Comparing the figures between 1981 and 1998-99, a reduction in income inequalities between the provinces is evident. This was possible due to the slowdown in Sindh's economy, along with buoyancy in the other provinces. NWFP has shown rapid progress during the period, which can be attributed to the large inflow of aid following the war in Afghanistan, boom of NGOs that brought in billions of dollars and, finally, remittances. The largest number of migrants to Gulf countries from Pakistan came from NWFP and remittances completely transformed the economic, political and social landscape of NWFP. Favourable policy decisions in the late 1970s and 1980s gave an impetus to Punjab's economy as well.

Poverty

A study conducted by the Social Policy and Development Centre reveals there are significant differences in the regional incidence of poverty. The report *Social Development in Pakistan, Annual Review 2000*, gives a number of interesting insights:

- Balochistan is the most poverty-stricken province in the country, with the highest incidence of both rural and urban poverty.
- Sindh has the second highest incidence of poverty at 27 per cent. The poverty gap between urban and rural Sindh are also very high.
- Rural Sindh and Balochistan suffer acute poverty.
- The incidence of poverty is lowest in NWFP
- Punjab is the only province where poverty is more pervasive in the urban than in the rural areas, explained by the vibrant agricultural base of the provincial economy.

Poverty incidence has only increased since 1996-97 in Pakistan, touching a high 32 per cent in 2002.

Development Parameters

Household Profile

Large differences are observed among provinces in terms of household amenities. Not only does Punjab have the highest concentration of household units, it leads in terms of amenities provided too. Over 72 per cent of the households in the province are electrified, 42 per cent receive tap water and 32 per cent use gas. These levels are higher than the national average and also outperform all other provinces.

Among the provinces, Balochistan is least developed. Only 14 per cent of the households have concrete or *pucca* houses, while the national average is much higher at 55 per cent. The province is also the least electrified with only 47 per cent of the households receiving power. Balochistan has the largest gas reserves and is the second largest producer of gas in the country, but consumes hardly 17 per cent of the gas produced. This is reflected in the fact that only 10 per cent of households receive gas as cooking fuel.

In terms of household amenities and development, Punjab is most developed, followed by Sindh and NWFP in close competition. Balochistan trails far behind.

Income Poverty : An Inter-provincial Comparision, 1996-97

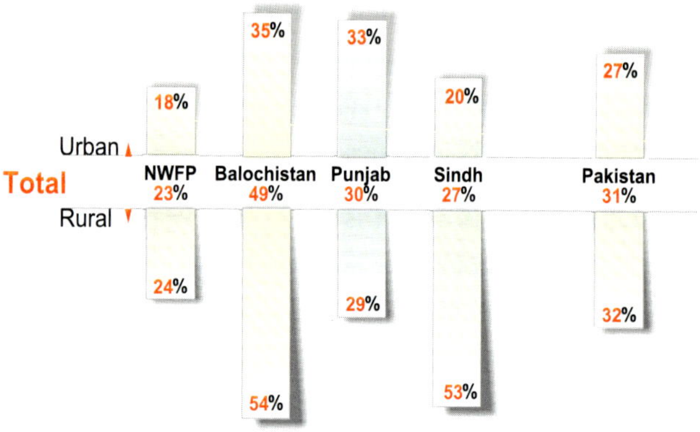

Source: Social Development in Pakistan. Annual Review 2000, Social Policy and Development Centre

Table 3.4: Human Development Index

	Urban	Rural	Overall
Punjab	0.657	0.517	0.557
Sindh	0.659	0.456	0.540
Balochistan	0.591	0.486	0.499
NWFP	0.627	0.489	0.510
Pakistan	-	-	0.541

Source: Pakistan National Human Development Report, 2003 UNDP

Human Development

Sindh urban ranks highest while Sindh rural has the lowest HDI. This only reflects wide intra-regional disparity. Punjab has the least disparity between its rural and urban areas. Amongst rural areas, Punjab rural has the highest HDI.

The HDI shows wide provincial variations from the highest in the Punjab at 0.557 to the lowest at 0.499 in Balochistan. Urban Balochistan is the least developed with the lowest index among urban areas. Similar is the case with rural Balochistan.

Observing the rural human development index, Punjab has the highest HDI of 0.517, followed by NWFP at a distant 0.489, followed by Balochistan at 0.489 and then Sindh at 0.456. This shows wide disparity in the development of rural Punjab and that of rural areas in other provinces.

Literacy

Pakistan's literacy rate has increased from 13 per cent in 1951 to almost 45 per cent in 2003. However, the education profile of literate Pakistan is not very impressive. Pakistan suffers from high dropout rates of 50 per cent post-primary schooling. Only 5-10 per cent of the children enrolled at the primary level complete schooling.

The Labour Force Survey, 2001-02, reveals that Pakistan's literacy levels were 50 per cent by end-2002. This implies that of a population of 146 million in 2002, 73 million were literate. Of these, 49 million were school dropouts, and barely four million (or 3 per cent of the total population) were graduates.

Amongst the provinces, Balochistan has the lowest literacy rate of 27 per cent. An inadequate educated class has greatly hampered Balochistan's potential for development. The local people are marginalized with migrants wresting control over key economic activities.

NWFP also suffers from poor literacy, with over 60 per cent of the population illiterate. Even among youth in the age-group of 15-34, literacy is hardly 40 per cent. Sindh and Punjab have the highest literacy rates of 47 per cent.

Pakistan's overall literacy is uninspiring. With government failing to provide quality formal education, a parallel system of education – the madrassas imparting Islamic values – are acting as cushion absorbing the spill-over mainly from the poorer classes. This dual system of education has spawned several ramifications:

- Lack of a uniform education system has divided society into religious and secular groups

Table 3.5: Household Profile

Indicators	Punjab	Sindh	Balochistan	NWFP	Pakistan
Number of Households (In million)	10.50	5.00	0.97	2.20	19.20
Household Size (Persons)	6.90	6.00	6.70	8.00	6.80
Pucca housing units (%)	62.00	46.69	14.19	56.15	54.64
Housing units with Electricity (%)	72.49	70.08	46.62	72.19	70.46
Housing units with tap water (%)	26.52	41.70	29.64	39.46	32.26
Housing units using gas (%)	17.67	32.43	9.84	9.80	20.19
Housing units with separate kitchen (%)	31.50	34.60	22.70	33.00	32.70
Housing units with separate latrine (%)	26.52	35.36	18.58	36.86	28.58

Source: Population Census Organisation, 1998, Pakistan Development Forum, Islamabad, 2003, Household Integrated Economic Survey, 2001-02

Table 3.6: Literacy 1998 Census

(Per cent)

Age-group	Balochistan	NWFP	Sindh	Punjab	Pakistan
10 & above	26.6	37.3	46.7	47.4	45.0
10-14	35.5	49.1	53.9	59.0	55.3
15-19	36.2	51.8	55.4	62.7	58.2
20-24	31.3	43.8	49.7	56.4	52.0
25-34	24.5	32.9	47.1	47.6	44.7
35-44	20.1	28.8	43.1	41.3	39.3
45-54	15.8	22.3	36.6	31.4	30.8
55 & above	10.3	15.5	28.6	21.0	21.5

Source: Pakistan Statistical Year Book, 2003

- It has failed to groom individuals and has promoted a faceless *jihadi* mindset
- It has aggravated discrimination on the basis of the financial stature of individuals.

Youth Profile & Employment

About 19 per cent of Pakistan's population constitute the youth, numbering 25 million people. Punjab evidently has the highest concentration of 56 per cent of the youth population, followed by Sindh. Between them, the two provinces shelter over 80 per cent of the youth population of Pakistan. Balochistan accounts for hardly five per cent, while NWFP 14 per cent.

Illiteracy amongst the youth of Pakistan is a matter of concern. Hardly 55 per cent or 14 million youth are literate, of which around 7 million would have dropped out at the primary level itself. Hardly half-a-million are graduates. Also, 45 per cent of the youth are illiterate. This reflects the poor quality of Pakistan's youth. On this count, Punjab, which houses the country's largest proportion of youth, is worst affected. According to the 1998 Census, there are over 5.6 million illiterate youth in Punjab accounting for over 40 per cent of the province's total youth population. A similar trend can be seen in Sindh where 47 per cent of the youth are uneducated. But the worst affected provinces are Balochistan and NWFP with respective shares of 66 per cent and 52 per cent of illiterate youth population.

As per the 1998 Census, there are about 29 million people in the working age-group of 20-34 years. Based on the national activity rate ranging from 51 to 54 per cent for these age-groups, it leads to about 15 million people being employed and the remaining 14 million being unemployed. A large fraction of this unemployed young working group is concentrated in Punjab and Sindh.

Agricultural Mechanisation

Punjab, with the largest area under cultivation, is also far ahead in terms of farm mechanisation and use of other inputs. Tractor penetration in the province is deep with 58 hectares per tractor. Mechanisation in Sindh, the second agricultural province of Pakistan, is relatively low, with a ratio of 253 hectares per tractor. NWFP province seems relatively better placed with 128 hectares per tractor. The worst level of mechanisation is in Balochistan.

In terms of input for agriculture, per hectare fertiliser consumption in Punjab is highest. Over 67 per cent of the total fertiliser consumption in Pakistan is in Punjab alone. Around 0.16 tonnes of fertilisers is used per hectare of area cultivated. Sindh is the second highest consumer of fertiliser with a usage of 0.11 tonnes per hectare cultivated. While NWFP's fertiliser consumption is comparable to Sindh's, Balochistan is the weakest with 0.03 tonnes per hectare.

Table 3.7: Use of Tractors

	Total Tractors (numbers)	Cultivated Area (mln hectares)	Penetration (hectares per tractor)
Punjab	210,628	12.31	58
Sindh	23,182	5.87	253
NWFP	14,571	1.87	128
Balochistan	4,480	2.07	462
Pakistan	252,861	22.12	87

Source: Pakistan Statistical Yearbook, 2002-03

Urban Centres

The 1998 census reported Pakistan's urban population to be 42.46 million, growing at 3.5 per cent per annum over the 1981-98 inter-censal period: the official urban population of Pakistan, as a percentage of total population, has gone up

Table 3.8: Youth Profile (Age-group 15-24 years)

	Youth (mln nos)	Illiterate Youth (mln nos)	% Share of Youth to total youth pop	% Share of Illiterates to total prov. youth pop
Balochistan	1.24	0.82	5.0	66.2
NWFP	3.36	1.75	13.6	52.2
Sindh	5.99	2.84	24.2	47.5
Punjab	13.93	5.64	56.4	40.5
Pakistan	24.69	11.08	100.0	44.9

Source: Pakistan Statistical Year Book, 2003 (minor diff in totals)

from approximately 18 per cent to over 32 per cent since 1951. For the period 1972-81 and 1981-98, the urban growth rates in Sindh, Punjab and NWFP have been similar at around 3.5 per cent per annum. However, each province has a distinct urbanisation pattern, reflecting mainly the traditional provincial hierarchies.

A study carried out by Haroon Jamal and Amir Jahan Khan of the Social and Policy Development Centre, Pakistan, observes that nearly 58 per cent of Pakistan's districts fall in the category of low development. Only twelve districts in the country can be classified as highly developed regions, of which eight lie in Punjab alone.

Balochistan and NWFP show very poor development with only one highly developed district each. Conditions in Balochistan are worst; 24 out of 26 districts are poorly developed.

The high-developed districts in Punjab are Lahore, Rawalpindi, Sialkot, Jhelum, Gujranwala, Faisalabad, Gujrat and T.T.Singh. Those of Sindh include Karachi and Hyderabad. NWFP and Balochistan have Peshawar and Quetta respectively.

Clearly, Balochistan has been a traditional laggard. With hardly five per cent of Pakistan's population located in this province, developmental activities have never received due priority.

A study conducted by Haroon Jamal and Amir Jahan Khan in *The Changing Profile of Regional Inequality*, April 2003 (SPDC), observes:

- Overall, Pakistan has experienced a widening in inequality during 1981-1998.
- Regional inequality is the highest in Balochistan, followed by NWFP and Sindh. It is lowest in Punjab.
- Except for Punjab, inequality has increased in all the other three provinces from 1981 to 1998.
- Inequality has increased due to unequal development of indicators related to agriculture, manufacturing, labour force, bank branches and number of cars.
- Balochistan has continued to fall behind the rest of the country during the last 20 years.
- In Sindh, except for Karachi and Hyderabad, all other districts are at the low or middle level of development.
- Districts of Punjab have generally improved their position.
- NWFP appears to be acquiring the characteristics of an emerging economy. Going by above parameters for prosperity, the following facts can be garnered:
- Balochistan's economy has stagnated since the past two decades. Human conditions have deteriorated while disparities within the province have widened.
- NWFP has shown rapid progress, but is still a long way from growing into a developed economy. Human conditions are improving while the economy is also showing dynamism. However, most of the growth in the province in the past two decades has come merely from easy money, rather than strong fundamentals.

- Sindh was the most progressive region till 1970s. However, since then the economy has suffered a major setback. Sindh's development has been in and around Karachi, while the other parts seem to have been neglected. Disparities between rural and urban Sindh are very high.
- Punjab has been the most rapidly growing economy in all terms, with overall development in the rural and urban areas alike. Industrialisation has generally received the thrust. Considering that it is the most populous province, it has still managed to remain on the growth track probably due to a boost received through conscious policy decisions.

Table 3.9: Distribution of Districts in Development Levels: 1998

	Development level			
	High	Middle	Low	Total
Balochistan	1	1	24	26
NWFP	1	8	15	24
Sindh	2	5	9	16
Punjab	8	16	10	34
Pakistan	12	30	58	100

Source: *Changing Profile of Regional Inequality,* by Haroon Jamal and Amir Jahan Khan, SPDC

Economic Activities/Contribution to National Economy

In Pakistan, rather than entire provinces, it is smaller regions or zones, which should be seen as hubs of industrial activity. Karachi is always such a region where FDI would be lucrative; the Lahore-Faisalabad-Gujranwalla in central Punjab zone is another, as is the Peshawar-Mardan-Nowshera region in the NWFP. In terms of economic development, there are vibrating exceptions in an otherwise placid country

Agriculture

Pakistan's economy is primarily driven by the agriculture sector. The country is endowed with good fertile land and water resources, with the largest contiguous irrigation system in the world. Performance of the farm sector has varied significantly over the years. Growth has come from different sources in different periods: a seed, fertiliser and irrigation package in the 1960s, intensification of water and fertiliser use in the 1970s, and improvement in crop management in the 1980s.

However, in the past decade, especially in the latter half of 1990s, growth in agriculture has distinctly slowed down.

Punjab is the backbone of the agricultural economy of Pakistan. It contributes about 68 per cent to annual food grain production in the country. Cotton and Basmati rice are its major produce, exports of which contribute substantially to the national exchequer.

Sindh is the second highest contributor to the agriculture sector. NWFP and Balochistan are poor contributors to foodgrain production. However, the two excel in production of cash crops – tobacco and fruits respectively – that have been major revenue earners.

Industry/Manufacturing

Pakistan has developed a modest industrial base in steel, textiles, sugar, cement, leather goods, chemicals plastics and few other items.

Nevertheless, Pakistan greatly lacks industrialisation. Most industrial development in Pakistan is in the area of agro-based industries or consumer goods.

The growth rate of the manufacturing sector has been 8.2 per cent in 2000-01, 5 per cent in 2001-02 and 7.7 in 2002-03. This may seem impressive in light of more recent trends, but in 1999-00 the manufacturing growth rate was only 1.5 per cent. Whatever growth there has been in manufacturing has been based on earlier poor performance. What is more important is the fact that total investment, both private and public in the three years from 2000-01 onwards has been the lowest in the last fifty years!!

Pakistan's business houses are much smaller compared to international standards and operate in niche markets. Also, there is a larger and more visible presence of multinationals, which are well established and control key sectors.

In the 1960s and early 1970s, there were about 50 firms that dominated Pakistan's business, industrial and financial sectors.

Table 3.10: Province-wise Production of Crops: 1999-2000

	Area 000 Hec	Production 000 Tonnes	Yield kg/ha	% share of production to total production
Wheat				
Punjab	6180	16480	2667	78.2
Sindh	1144	3001	2623	14.2
NWFP	807	1068	1324	5.1
Balochistan	332	530	1595	2.5
Pakistan	8463	21079	2491	100.0
Rice				
Punjab	1609	2481	1541	48.1
Sindh	690	2123	3075	41.2
NWFP	67	129	1925	2.5
Balochistan	149	422	2844	8.2
Pakistan	2515	5155	2050	100.0
Cotton				
Punjab	2329	2329	881	84.9
Sindh	633	405	822	14.8
NWFP	0.3	0.1	340	0.0
Balochistan	20	10	493	0.4
Pakistan	2982	2744	941	100.0
Sugarcane				
Punjab	672	27081	42300	58.4
Sindh	231	14291	62000	30.8
NWFP	106	4917	46300	10.6
Balochistan	1	43	54300	0.1
Pakistan	1010	46332	64000	100.0
Maize				
Punjab	411	717	1986	46.2
Sindh	9	5	535	0.3
NWFP	539	827	1534	53.3
Balochistan	3	3	1120	0.2
Pakistan	962	1552	1718	100.0
Pulses				
Punjab	1096	620	566	77.3
Sindh	211	133	630	16.6
NWFP	87	32	368	4.0
Balochistan	25	18	720	2.2
Pakistan	1419	802	565	100
Fruits				
Punjab	353	3573	10122	61.1
Sindh	108	774	7167	13.2
NWFP	47	541	11511	9.3
Balochistan	149	958	6430	16.4
Pakistan	657	5846	8898	100
Vegetables				
Punjab	2014	129	64	69.7
Sindh	212	35	165	7.3
NWFP	333	31	93	11.5
Balochistan	331	24	73	11.5
Pakistan	2889	218	75	100

Source: National Fertiliser Development Centre-Pakistan, (http://www.fadinap.org/pakistan)

Most were family firms and were well known: Habibs, Dawoods, Adamjees, Isphanis, Saigols, etc. However, very few of these business houses exist today. The market in their time was narrow and these firms had grown in a highly protected market. They were strong vertically but did not have a horizontal spread. These business houses generally operated in exclusive areas but jointly covered Pakistan's key economic sectors.

Nationalisation during Bhutto's regime in 1970s helped loosen the hold of this powerful coterie. However, it promoted alliances among the state bureaucracy, large landowners, nascent industrialists and the army – extending privileges to each other and in the process grabbing control over economic resources. Things have changed since with the emergence of first generation entrepreneurs.

Today, the market is far wider due to demographic changes, urbanisation, consumerism, and growing transparency. There are perhaps thousand business houses operating in Pakistan, where there were only 50. Traditional business houses of Pakistan operated in a veil of secrecy and generally recoiled from conforming to disclosure practices. Their true net worth or their investments abroad were never fully known, resulting in only a fuzzy picture of their operations being available to the general public. Evasion of taxes and other forms of disclosure is rampant amongst Pakistani firms – differentiated here from multinational corporations – and with occasional drives of accountability, as was in the case of the Moeen Quraishi caretaker government of three months in 1993, and again under the still functioning National Accountability Bureau set up when General Musharraf took over, many business houses have tried to keep a low profile.

There are nevertheless some business houses that have emerged since 1980. Nawaz Sharief's Ittefaq Empire, engaged in numerous industries including steel, chemicals and trading, is most prominent. Then there are the Chaudhry's of Gujrat, who are the backbone of Musharraf's PML(Q). Amongst the more business minded, not directly in politics like the Chaudhrys or Nawaz Sharief, are a number of houses which are based largely on textiles. This traditional sector still continues to be the main avenue through which firms and houses have become established, although that is now changing due to a growing domestic consumer market in Pakistan, where things like mineral water, eatables, consumer products, etc, are gaining popularity.

The groups which have grown in recent years are the Saphire Group in the Punjab, in textiles and now garments and diversifying into other areas; Chenab Group, high value added garments both for the domestic market and on exports, now moving in to leasing; Nagina, into textiles, finance, weaving, garments; Babar Ali, old money made from construction in the 1950s and 1960s, now diversified and 'modernised' into consumer products having captured many urban consumer products like mineral water, biscuits, etc, in joint partnership with Nestles – also owns and set up LUMS, the Lahore University of Management Sciences. There is the current Commerce Minister Humayun Akhtar Khan, son of the former ISI chief, who received huge sums of money when he headed the ISI against the Afghans. All these groups are Lahore based; many of the Pakistani businessmen in the large category are in garments and are from the Chinioti *biradari*. In Karachi, Yousuf Shirazi is the motorcycle king of Pakistan and has had a near monopoly of motorcycle production of Atlas/Honda motorcycles; the Lakhanis, Ismailis, migrants from Bombay, started in tobacco but now own McDonalds, much of the tobacco market in Pakistan, consumer products like detergents and toothpaste, etc, and surgical exports, also in textiles. The

Table 3.11: Registered Companies: 2003

Companies incorporated	43,618
Public listed cos	687
Public non-listed cos	2,214
Private cos: ltd by share	39,628
Trade cos: ltd by guarantee	83
Unlimited cos	6
Welfare Org./Associations	357
Foreign cos	643

Source: Board of Investments, Government of Pakistan.

Hashwanis also Ismailis, are in trading, hotels, leasing, etc. Much of industry in Pakistan has been located in the central Punjab and Sindh while some in the NWFP, very little in Balochistan.

Although Pakistan's business environment is generally favourable, business houses tend to shy away from domestic investment. Firstly, it is the threat to life emanating from the intermittent bouts of violence and unrest, and secondly, it is the fear of having to comply with accounting norms that are often imposed abruptly and have incriminating consequences. Whenever banks publish a list of defaulting borrower companies, business houses run for cover, swearing never to invest in Pakistan. There is another limiting factor; business houses that are politically sponsored run the risk of being victimized when there is a shift in political regime.

This political victimisation is clearly evident in the case of Karachi. Till the early 1970s, Karachi was the hub of industrialisation in Pakistan. However, post Bhutto-regime of Zia-ul-Haq, Sindh turned politically volatile resulting in a major shift of manufacturing industries from Karachi to Punjab. Karachi has been at the centre of political, ethnic, and sectarian violence since 1985 and has seen its economy crumble under the weight of these problems. Investment flows into Sindh have slowed down, and there is evidence of a shift in investment destination to Punjab and Dubai.

Up to 1978, the number of companies incorporated in Karachi every year exceeded that of Punjab. In the first year of General Zia's rule in 1978-79, 273 companies were incorporated in Punjab against 275 in Karachi. For the next three years, Karachi and Punjab were in fierce competition. In 1982, for the first time the annual incorporation of companies in Punjab exceeded that of Karachi.

This is also confirmed by the location of companies listed on stock exchanges. In 1997, of the total 550 listed companies engaged in manufacturing activities, only 184 were located in Karachi and Sindh, of which 91 were incorporated in the pre-Bhutto era. On the other hand, only 44 of the 250 listed companies engaged in manufacturing activities in Punjab belonged to that era. This is indicative of the shift of industries from Sindh to Punjab, and the relative industrial expansion of Punjab in the post-Bhutto regime.

According to the 1995-96 Census on Manufacturing Industries, there were around 4,474 reporting establishments in Pakistan. Over 30 per cent of these industries were in the textile sector followed by another 20 per cent engaged in food manufacturing. This clearly reflects the high dominance of agro-based industries in Pakistan's manufacturing segment.

Region-wise, 52 per cent of the industries were located in Punjab while 34 per cent were in Sindh. NWFP had around 600 to its credit, while Balochistan had a very absence of the manufacturing sector.

Revenue Generation and Contribution

In Pakistan, almost 90 per cent of the revenue is collected at the federal level, and the remaining 10 per cent assembled between the two lower tiers of the government -provincial and local. An elaborate mechanism exists by which fiscal transfers from the federal to the provincial governments take place from taxes collected by the former. The Constitution of 1973 has established a basic framework for the division of powers and the distribution of revenues between the federation and the provinces.

Table 3.12: Assigned Shares to Provinces Under NFC Awards

(% share)

Years	1970	1974	1990	1997
Balochistan	2	4	5	5
NWFP	16	13	14	14
Sindh	23	23	23	23
Punjab	57	60	58	58

Source: Nuzhat Ahmad and Syed Ashraf Wasti of Applied Economic Research Centre, Karachi

Under the Constitution, the federal government and the provinces have access to a divisible pool comprising the net proceeds of specified taxes, in addition to their exclusive sources of revenues.

In this regard, the National Finance Commission (NFC) is constituted by the President every five years, which is meant to devise a revenue-sharing formula for the divisible pool. In the last constituted NFC in 1997, it was decided to give 37.5 per cent of the total divisible pool to the provinces, while 62.5 per cent would be retained by the federal government. The NFC in 2003 had decided to equally share the proceeds between the province and federal government. The transfers to the provinces amount to about 6 per cent of GDP. The divisible pool comprises of direct taxes (including income and corporation tax), sales duty, excise duty, export duties, import duties, estate/succession duties, capital value tax on immovable properties, petroleum surcharge and gas development surcharge.

The revenue is shared between provinces on the basis of population. As a result, Punjab receives the maximum share from the divisible pool, followed by Sindh, NWFP and Balochistan.

With most revenue collection happening at the federal level, the federal government is always in surplus while the provincial governments are always saddled with budgetary deficits. As a result, provinces are not financially self-reliant and fill the gap through intergovernmental transfers from the federal to the provincial governments. In the process, the provinces also accumulate central debt.

Punjab and Sindh are able to finance about 18-20 per cent of their expenditure. The remaining coming in the form of foreign funds and federal transfers. NWFP also faces a similar situation being able to finance about 10-12 per cent of its expenditure. The most dismal fiscal position is that of Balochistan, which relies on the federal government for about 95 per cent of its expenses.

In terms of provincial contributions to the national exchequer, it is Sindh that leads. Thanks to the all-important Karachi seaport, the province's said contribution is 68 per cent. However, the province is highly discriminated in terms of transfers, getting hardly 23 per cent of the gross provincial transfers.

In this set up, Punjab proves to be a major beneficiary, receiving much more than its contribution. Its input to the national exchequer, in terms of taxes collected, is hardly 23 per cent but withdraws over 56 per cent from the divisible pool's share for provinces. Punjab not only receives a major share from the taxes redistributed among the provinces, the civil and military bureaucracy being mainly Punjabi, it gets a large share of the government budget which is also re-ploughed into the province.

NWFP and Balochistan are very small beneficiaries and their accruals are relatively proportionate to their contribution to the exchequer.

Sindh's case is rather peculiar. Most of its revenue is generated in and around Karachi, while most of remaining Sindh is highly backward. Though its contribution has been substantial at 68 per cent of total revenues, the benefit accrued in terms of transfer of funds has been rather small. It receives hardly 23 per cent of the funds disbursed to provinces. Karachi's development is self-oriented, being the commercial hub, but remaining parts of Sindh have hardly grown.

NWFP and Balochistan have continued to remain backward - acute paucity of funds, internal or external has resulted in widespread under-development.

Table 3.13: Taxes Collected From and Paid to the Provinces (1991-92 to 1995-96)

	Taxes Collected		Share Paid	
	Rs billion	% share	Rs billion	% share
Balochistan	38	4.29	18	5.27
NWFP	42	4.71	45	13.51
Sindh	619	69.45	78	23.13
Punjab	192	21.55	194	58.09

Source: *Sindh's case for a better NFC deal*, by Mohammad Anwar and Raza Haroon, Business Recorder, September 5, 2003

Conclusion

Punjab's overwhelming domineering perception has led to the belief that the overarching Punjabi identity is undermining the linguistic and ethnic identities of other groups, thus creating deep resentments against Punjab and the federal government. Moreover, with the military and bureaucracy coming from here acts as a potent force.

Pakistan has had a natural base for agriculture with diversification into secondary and tertiary sectors not receiving serious thrust. Punjab, owing to its conducive geographical conditions has been the fulcrum of Pakistan's agriculture. Industry sector rests on agriculture and hence the continuing dependence.

Punjab-domination has fuelled discontent among the smaller provinces since the 1970s. All economic statements and policies have remained contentious in light of this dominance. The smaller provinces have been dissatisfied with the distribution of power and resources between the provinces and the federal government, which has immeasurably benefited Punjab.

The smaller provinces perceive maximum autonomy as the way out of Punjab's domination. Provincial autonomy dominates the manifestos of several smaller political parties. This argument has garnered a great deal of force in recent years and has got intertwined with the motives of several ethnic separatist groups across the provinces like the Pakistan Oppressed Nations Movement (PONM), Jiye Sindh Quami Mahaz, Awami National Party, etc.

At the PONM rally held on May 17, 2004, organised in Quetta, the leaders stated: "Punjab must accept the rights of the oppressed nationalities because continuous denial of the constitutional and political rights of Balochs, Sindhis and Seraikis would harm the integrity of the country." Already political rallies in 2004 are reflecting an impulsion in anti-Punjab rhetoric and references to the 1971 situation in Pakistan. Moreover, in the first five months of 2004, Balochistan witnessed 5 major bomb blasts particularly targeting gas pipelines en route to Punjab.

Since 2004, there has been intensification in activities of smaller political groups, especially in Sindh and Balochistan – mobilising to collectively fight Punjab's domination. Initiation of contentious development projects, distribution of water resources, royalty, the National Finance Commission allocations, all have become issues of debate and are laying the foundations for increasing agitations among the smaller groups.

Such a situation has the potential to provide a thrust to separatist activities, signs of which are already visible though in a nascent stage. There is little doubt now that many Sindh-speaking people and Balochis are feeling alienated in the present federal structrure. The army however has had a track record of suppressing Balochi, Sindhi, Seraiki and Mohajir agitations in the past with a brutal combination of force and manipulation. Further, it has been these very agitations that have provided legitimacy to the army to remain in power. Some politicians and intellectuals propose restructuring of the provinces to divert attention.

People of Pakistan can obviously see through them since the same lobbies support manipulation by the army. A resurgence of nationalist forces in the smaller deprived provinces will once again consolidate the position of the military in Pakistani polity. But, the gravity of the situation within the provinces and the alliance forged by the separatist groups across provinces would be the determining factor for Pakistan's unity. Individual separatist groups in provinces will not be in a position to challenge a brutal military power. The coming together of groups from various provinces, particularly from Sindh and Balochistan, will pose a threat to overall Punjabi-domination and the supremacy of the military.

The survival of Pakistan for even a decade longer will be challenging in light of the degree of strength and weakness possessed by the Punjabi unitarists and provincial separatists.

CHAPTER 4

Balochistan

Balochistan received provincial status on July 1, 1970, when the former administrative divisions of Quetta and Kalat were merged. It is located in western Pakistan, and is bordered by Afghanistan on the northwest, Iran on the west and the Arabian Sea on the south. The province shares its borders with the other three provinces of Pakistan, with Punjab and Sindh to the east and the tribal area of North West Frontier Province (NWFP) in the north.

Spread over an area of approximately 347,641 sq km, Balochistan is the largest province covering over 43 per cent of the total geographical area. Though largest in terms of area, it is the least populated housing just five per cent of the population. Seventy per cent of the country's coastline lies in this province. The landscape here is mainly mountainous with barren and rugged terrain and marked by a diverse environment. Sixty-five per cent of Balochistan's area is rangeland and only 5 per cent is arable.

Much of prehistoric Balochistan's vast area is now divided between Iran, Pakistan and Afghanistan. During the era of British India, combined Balochistan commanded a strategic position in terms of being a principal trade route between South-West Asia, Central Asia and South Asia. Its significance was not only economic, but also strategic and geopolitical. As a result, Colonial Britain entered into a treaty with the Khan, ruler of Balochistan, in order to defend its western frontiers. At the same time, the Iranian rulers, who had lost their northern provinces to Russia, pursued a policy of expansion towards Balochistan in order to compensate for the lost areas. British India, in order to please Iran and keep away the Russians, decided to accept the demand of Iranians. Following intense negotiations between 1870 and 1900, Balochistan was divided into three parts, shared between Iran, Afghanistan and the then British India.

At the time of Pakistan's formation, Balochistan was divided into two areas which included the British Balochistan comprising of Pushto speaking tribal areas and the native Balochistan comprising of the erstwhile states of Kalat, Kharan and Bela. These two areas became part of Pakistan and were merged into One-Unit in 1955. Later, with the abolition of the unitary system in West Pakistan, in 1970, Balochistan received complete provincial status. However, even after the elections of December 1970, Balochistan continued to remain under Central rule until the first provincial assembly was convened in April 1972.

Along with the formation of the new state came reservations among the local populace of under-representation in local governance. This fuelled a major insurgency lasting for four years from 1973 to 1977. The people of Balochistan have waged guerrilla struggle ever since the British left, but this long dormant crisis erupted into a brutal confrontation with the centre in 1973. Fresh with the experience of losing East Pakistan, the Bhutto government decided to viciously curb the insurgency with the help of the Pakistani army who deployed over 80,000 troops and employed brutal methods and superior firepower, especially air attacks, with the help of the Iranians. Some 55,000 Pakistani Balochs were involved in the insurgency, of which 11,500 were organised combatants. This war consumed 3,300 Pakistani soldiers and 5,300 Baloch guerrillas.

The Baloch were not fighting for independence but rather for regional autonomy – the primary grievance was the influx of Punjabi settlers. Violence broke out in the province following an attack upon Goth Mohammad Hussain, a village dominated by Punjabi settlers in the Pat Feeder area in Katch district, by about thousand local tribesmen, in December 1972.

The timing for the insurgency move was inopportune as it closely succeeded a radical restructuring of Pakistan. In the aftermath of the Bengali secession, it was difficult to impartially judge Balochis' demands. During the Bhutto regime, hostilities with Balochistan were protracted, but the succeeding military ruler, General Zia-ul-Haq, adopted a more moderate approach, relying on economic development to placate the Baloch people.

However, by the time the attacks subsided in 1977, separatist feelings had intensified. Another outcome of admitting a military operation in Balochistan was providing the military with an opportunity to once again dabble in politics, which had in fact eroded after its debacle in 1971. On the pretext that the civil government was incapable of maintaining law and order, the army could prepare for a more comprehensive role. Prime Minister Zulfikar Ali Bhutto, in his book, '*If I am Assasinated*', stated that he was unable to withdraw the army on several occasions from Balochistan during the period of insurgency.

After over three decades, Balochistan still continues to struggle for its rights, resorting to violence as their only expression of dissent. The province has remained the least developed and also among the poorest. In spite of being rich in mineral resources and having a low population, Balochis lead a life of privation.

Balochistan, since its merger with Pakistan, has witnessed three armed conflicts in 1948, 1958 and in 1973. The later two events were basically reactions of an ethnic group perceiving the threat of subjugation. The root cause lay in the unfulfilled aspirations for an autonomous state.

Nevertheless, the social order is to blame for the province's restricted economic development. People have chosen to remain closed self-contained tribal groups, insular and even hostile to external influence. This has vitiated developmental prospects.

Social Structure

Balochistan has a predominantly tribal structure headed by *Sardars* (chief of the tribe) who rule with varying degrees of stringency. These tribal chiefs are very powerful and wield tremendous power to even challenge the state. Their society is structured on kinship and the main tribal heads are determined by heredity.

There are about 400 different tribes in the province with as many *Sardars*, with 18 major tribes, the most prominent and largest being the Marris and Bugtis. The inhabitants of Balochistan can be classified into three major ethnic groups – the Baloch, the Pathan and the Brahui – with several other smaller ethnic groups; all of which are divided into tribes. There are numerous other smaller tribes like the Mengal, Powandas, Wazir, Mazari and Mandokhels, to name a few.

Ethnic and tribal identity is a potent force for both individuals and groups in Balochistan with the result that there exists deep polarisation among different groups. Each of these groups is based on different rules of social organisation, which has left the province inexorably fragmented. This structure has stifled economic development of the region, where these tribes have remained self-sufficient agrarian communities with neither administrative ties nor major economic exchange of goods and services. Tribal groupism has failed to integrate the state and enforce a national identity. Moreover, it is in the interest of the *Sardars* to buttress the feelings of rivalry and exclusivity, in order to retain control.

These tribals are heavily armed and deploy missiles and rocket propelled grenades as a matter of routine. This has engendered lawlessness and vulnerability, which instigates massive violence at the slightest provocation. The deweaponisation drive undertaken in Pakistan in 2000-2001 could not penetrate 93 per cent of Balochistan.

None of the political and military leaders of Pakistan have displayed the will to eliminate the *Sardari* system. Following the insurgency in 1973-77, the Bhutto government in its final years had tried to abolish the *Sardari* system with the aim to disempower the *Sardars*. However, these reforms were nullified by General Zia ul Haq. Only in 2003, following a series of law and order problems in the aftermath of 9/11, was any serious attempt made to reorganise Balochistan.

Over the years, the role of *Sardars* has transformed from being merely the defender of his tribe to one of mediator between the tribe and the state. This was most evident during 2002, when a series of acts of sabotage targeting national assets, with a view to antagonise Punjab and the federal government, was witnessed in Balochistan.

This anachronistic tribal structure has left Balochistan greatly underdeveloped. Their structure in reality has led to formation of fiefdoms, behaving like states having their own code of organisation, judiciary and security. These tribes owe allegiance only to their chiefs and have scant deference for Pakistan as a state.

Apart from being firmly rooted in tribalism, Balochistan still carries the legacy of the British after over 55 years of independence. One such case is the demarcation of 'A' and 'B' areas for law and order purposes. An 'A' area is where the provincial police rules while the 'B' areas are governed by a force called 'Levies' which are recruited on tribal basis. This system has helped *Sardars* to maintain and even increase their stranglehold over their domain.

Every district in Balochistan, to date, is divided into 'A' and 'B' areas. The major towns, mostly the district headquarter constitute the 'A' area while the rest of the district makes up the 'B' area. Every district has its own Levies force with every tribe in the district receiving a fixed number of seats. No person is eligible for joining the Levies without belonging to a tribe of the area.

The 'B' areas of Balochistan cover over 75 per cent of the total land area of the province. This system, set up in the British regime, is being followed till date and legitimises tribals to remain in power in their respective domain. These 'B' areas have today become a safe haven for law-breakers, as there is hardly any police penetration. With the existence of such a wide lawless tribal belt, development is bound to be hindered. Not surprising that the deweaponisation drive in Balochistan could not penetrate most parts of the province.

In the past, there has been little effort to deconstruct this system and allow civil institutions to govern the province. Attempts to bring the Baloch population into the mainstream through development efforts have come to naught. A neglected province, they continue to follow their tribal traditions, considering land their primary asset and cannot tolerate its encroachment by any other ethnic group. This constraining traditional value system has only entrenched Balochistan further into its primordial state, militating against any effort to develop the province or even integrating the population into the national mainstream.

A welcome change is on the anvil. The upcoming Gwadar port and the newly-discovered mineral resources have brought the region into focus and improved the investment climate. However, even these development projects are facing impediments from the local population, arising from a feared loss of identity and usurping of resources by external ethnic groups.

Following the tribal antagonism to local projects undertaken by the federal government and the 9/11 event bringing these areas into focus, General Musharraf announced in early December 2003, a plan to convert the 'B' areas into 'A' areas in a span of five years. In order to accomplish this objective, the government was setting up a Balochistan constabulary comprising of 6,000 local cadets. The government seems resolute in its intent, for by early 2004, the government had already managed to convert the Nasirabad constituency of Prime Minister Mir Zafarullah Khan Jamali, Lasbela constituency of the chief minister Jam Mohammad Yousuf and the outskirts of Quetta. However, these were areas that were easily accessible as their leaders were already part of mainstream politics.

A principal reason for the hitherto neglect of this province by the federal government in allocating funds for development could be ascribed to the fact that hardly 5 per cent of Pakistan's population is concentrated in Balochistan. As a result, on no account could the province merit central attention and resources. This has left the province lacking in both human and capital resources.

Population

Balochistan's population increased from about 2.4 million in 1972 to 7.4 million in 2003, and is likely to touch 8.7 million by 2010. The population growth rate has declined from an average of over 6 per cent during the inter-census period of 1972-1981 to 2.4 per cent during the period 1981-1998. However, the sudden jump in population in the inter-census period of 1972-81 can also be attributed to the large influx of Afghan refugees.

A quarter of the population in the province live in urban areas. However, urbanisation is very poor being limited to Quetta. The ratio of urban population to total provincial population went up from 16 per cent in 1981 to 24 per cent in 1998. Over 75 per cent of Balochistan's population lives in the rural areas. Half of the population is concentrated in close proximity to the capital city. Population is dense in Quetta, with approximately 255 people per sq km, Nasirabad with 80 people per sq km, Killa Abdullah with 74 people per sq km and Jaffarabad with a population density of 172 people per sq km. Population density in the remaining districts ranges from 3-35 people per sq km.

Balochis are the most dominant ethnic group comprising 55 per cent of the population, followed by Pushtos who constitute nearly 30 per cent. The Balochis are mostly spread over eastern and southern Balochistan, including the coastal belt. The Pashtuns are concentrated in Quetta, Zhob and the northern areas. Both these ethnic groups represent 85 per cent of the population of Balochistan and are politically competitive with conflicting aspirations for territorial adjustments. The province also has a sizeable number of Sindhi and Punjabi speaking people.

Table 4.1: Ethnic Composition of Balochistan

(% share)

	Urdu	Punjabi	Sindhi	Pushto	Baloch	Seraiki	Others
Total	0.98	2.52	5.58	29.64	54.76	2.42	4.12
Rural	0.21	0.43	5.27	32.16	57.56	1.87	2.51
Urban	3.42	9.16	6.57	21.61	45.84	4.16	9.24

The ethnic composition of Balochistan makes it extremely sensitive to ethnic violence. The Balochis and Pathans are considered archrivals; disputes over land and water rights are commonplace. Till the 1970s, the Balochis formed the predominant ethnic group in Balochistan. However, the ethnic composition underwent a marked change in the 1980s, when Afghan refugee camps comprising Pashtuns were set up in the northern parts of the province following the war in Afghanistan. These temporary settlements eventually transformed into *pucca* structures, staining the ethnic composition with Pashtuni colour. In 2003, there were 1.2 million Afghan refugees residing in Balochistan, accounting for 17 per cent of the local population.

Balochistan's demographic composition reflects a youthful structure with over 56 per cent of its population in the age-group of below 19 years. This vibrant population can be an asset for a state that needs major energetic efforts towards development. However, only 36 per cent of this youth population is literate, making it a rather ineffective tool to bring about social and political change.

As per the Census of 1998, youth population as defined in the age group of 15-24 years amounted to 1.24 million or 19 per cent of Balochistan's population. This age group had a literacy rate of 34 per cent. This implies that 66 per cent or 0.8 million in this age group were illiterate. Also, 50 per cent of students drop out even prior to completing primary level education, which means another 0.2 million hardly have basic education. Net result, out of 1.24 million youth in the province, one million are barely educated, and only quarter-of-a-million youth can make any significant contribution. Such a poor profile of its young population can be highly unfortunate as it reflects a vast degree of unskilled young manpower in the province that may find it difficult to progress beyond menial jobs.

The demographic profile of Balochistan is advantageous – a small population on a vast area rich in mineral resources. However, its bane lies in having a highly uneducated and unskilled manpower deeply rooted in tribal traditions. Further, except for relatively brief periods, the tribes in the province have never been united on a single national platform. Social interaction, as such, is poor given the difficult geographical terrain and the large physical distances between population clusters that cannot be bridged in the absence of communication facilities. Though the population will continue to rise at around 2.4 per cent per year for the remaining decade, its economy will be unable to keep pace unless a major internal restructuring occurs.

Economy

With a per capita income of $158 per year (Rs.9,144 @ of Rs.58/$) and two-thirds of its population engaged in primary activities, Balochistan possesses all the characteristics of an under-developed economy. Though largest in terms of geographical size, its economy is the smallest and least developed among the provinces of Pakistan. Balochistan's mineral resources have remained vastly untapped, proving to be more of academic than economic value.

Despite having the largest gas reserves in the country, it supplies over 80 per cent of its gas produce to Punjab and Sindh, while itself consumes hardly 17 per cent. According to the Household Integrated Economic Survey (HIES) of 2001-02, hardly 10 per cent of the households in Balochistan have gas connections. Further, only 1 per cent of the industrial gas consumers in the country are located in Balochistan. It is the least electrified region in the country with only 47 per cent of households thus benefiting.

Household amenities in the province are evidently insufficient. The HIES 2001-02 reveals that there are 9.7 lakh households in Balochistan with an average size of 6.7 persons per household. Of these, only 14 per cent of the houses were concrete as against a national average of 54.6 per cent. Only 30 per cent of them had tap water facilities while only 18 per cent had separate toilets. This implies that nearly 70 per cent of the population in the province are deprived of even basic amenities.

Approximately 3800 villages in Balochistan have no schools.

It also has the lowest enrolment rate in the country coupled with the highest drop out rate. According to the federal ministry of education, the total enrolment in Balochistan was 7.9 lakh students at all levels as against the total school going population of 19.6 lakh between the age group of 5-14 years. This implies that a large section of the population either avails of local religious schools – the *deeni madaris* – or remains uneducated.

Balochistan has the lowest health index as well. It has a high infant mortality rate of 82 deaths per thousand live births. The immunization ratio in Balochistan is as low as 34 per cent. Health facilities in the province are inhuman, with one hospital for over 1.6 lakh people. The doctor to people ratio is an appalling 1:5750. Medical practitioners are reluctant to practice in Balochistan due to poor working conditions. It was only in 1997 that the institute of public health was created to promote medical education and training facilities in Balochistan. The proportion of people having access to safe drinking water facilities in Balochistan is only 33 per cent.

Quetta and Ziarat are the only districts classified as developed, with the remaining 24 districts in the province falling in the low-development category. Most parts of this province have no access to the media. Balochistan also has an appalling railway and road network facility with mostly shingle roads.

Quetta clearly holds a very special position being the provincial capital. It is the hub of commercial and educational activities. The district has the highest literacy rate of 57 per cent. It has a high degree of urbanisation and the thickest population density. In terms of infrastructure, it has the largest concentration of metalled roads, and holds a central position in the communication network of the province. Interestingly, it is the third smallest district in Balochistan but plays a central role in the province.

Value of agricultural production

Ziarat, adjoining Quetta, is the smallest district in Balochistan with the smallest population and relatively low population growth rate. The district is a single crop area primarily producing fruits. This being a high value produce puts Ziarat in top position in terms of per capita value of agricultural production. The district reflects high enrolment figures. Literacy rate at 34.3 per cent is second highest and the district has the lowest number of illiterates. In terms of infrastructure, the district has the third highest and fifth highest density of metalled and shingle roads, respectively.

Balochistan is rich in mineral reserves. Besides significant ore deposits of gold, silver and copper, the province has the largest reserves of gas. However, the province has skimped on development initiatives. In the three decades of its formation, Balochistan had only three public sector projects to its credit – Sui Gas, Saindak Metals and Pak-Iran Textile Mills – resulting in Balochistan being a province with least federal government assets.

Much like population itself, industry in Balochistan is fragmented consisting of isolated independent units. Protection of this sparse capital is pursued almost as an obsession. There is no will to expand the industrial base, either by self or through external help. Investment intentions from other provinces into Balochistan are construed as threats that meet resentment and antagonism. Little does impoverished Balochistan realise that it needs to attract external investments to propel local economic development. Balochistan's best bargain is in mechanical farming and technology-intensive activities. However, not having enough capacity to generate the financial resources for such a transformation, these potential gains can be realised only through federal government and external participation. Export activities based on comparative advantage can also galvanize economic development.

Since 2002, much hope has been kindled by China's decision to invest in the Gwadar deep-sea port construction. This project is expected to bring much-needed economic and social transformation in the province – developing into a trade hub and a conduit to Central Asian Republics. The project has already brought Balochistan into international limelight.

Agriculture – the backbone

The primary economic activity pursued by a vast majority of the population is farming and livestock rearing. Agriculture is the mainstay of Balochistan's economy with over 60 per cent of the workforce linked directly or indirectly to this sector for its livelihood. Diverse agro-climatic conditions across the province permit cultivation of 65 different crops in both the Rabi and Kharif growing seasons. However, lack of water severely constrains agricultural development. Balochistan falls in the arid/semiarid zone with average annual precipitation ranging from 300-400 mm in the northwest to 75-100 mm in the southwest. Limited rainfall and water scarcity has restricted area under irrigation, to virtual absence.

Fruit production plays a vital role and has a share of 16 per cent in the country's total fruit production. Fruits being high-value products can help earn substantial foreign exchange. It is estimated that about 75 per cent of the total production of fruits in the province is indeed an exportable surplus. However, due lack of infrastructure and storage facilities, a large part of the produce perish. The upcoming Gwadar port can potentially help reverse this trend.

Table 4.2: Major Crops Grown in 2002

	Area (in hectares)	Production (in tonnes)
Fruits	129,700	1,431,000
Wheat	381,700	871,600
Rice	158,400	433,900
Vegetables	26,900	384,900
Barley	29,300	39,900
Jowar	23,500	23,100
Cotton	40,400	20,274
Maize	3,400	7,300

Source: *Balochistan Perspective*, May 2003 prepared by Pakistan Development Forum for the World Bank

At present, most of the fruits grown are exported to the other provinces of Pakistan, though there is enough demand from abroad but no infrastructure to tap these markets. Fruits mainly grown are dates, grapes, pomegranates, apples, almonds, apricots, plums, and peaches. The Loralai district of Balochistan is known as the 'Almond Bowl' of the country.

Being a pastoral region, livestock rearing is the other major activity in the province. Nearly 49 per cent of the total livestock population lies in Balochistan. As per the Livestock Census 1996, Balochistan had a livestock population of 27 million of which 50 per cent were sheep and 25 per cent goats. Livestock population in the province is much larger and outnumbers the human population.

Wheat, jowar and rice are Balochistan's major food crops, although their production is rather insignificant. Another allied agricultural activity is fishing – mainly in the coastal areas, especially Gwadar where over 80 per cent of the population comprises fishermen. Till 2002, fishing was more of a subsistence activity catering to local needs. However, several projects have been set up since with a view to enhance production and exports. In 2003, for instance, the Export Promotion Bureau started operations in Gwadar, with a view to promoting shrimp farming and its exports.

Agriculture, together with allied activities, forms the core of Balochistan's economy. In the 1970s, its contribution to the provincial GDP was 40 per cent, rising to 50 per cent in the 1980s. At present, Balochistan is a net exporter of fruits and vegetables, but a net importer of foodgrains. Balochistan's dream of finding its agriculture produce in the global markets might be fulfilled by the commissioning of the Gwadar port.

Since the late 1990s, Balochistan has been facing one of the worst droughts, which has had a debilitating impact on the agriculture sector. Drought conditions have been severe in 2000 and 2001. All the 23 districts of the province, barring the

Fishing Industry of Balochistan

Pat Feeder Canal fed district of Nasirabad and Jaffarabad and the coastal district of Gwadar, were declared as drought-affected. The eight districts most severely affected were located in northwest and central Balochistan.

The year 2003 saw suffering touch the other extreme. In a year of generally good rainfall in Pakistan, Balochistan had to indeed grapple with a floods calamity.

Water Resources of Balochistan

Falling in an arid/semi-arid zone, water scarcity in Balochistan has been historical. Surface and groundwater resources fluctuate greatly, depending on the precipitation. The province has no perennial river. Hence groundwater resources form a major source of water supply. There are an estimated 3,000 wells in Balochistan in addition to some 21,000 tube-wells, including a small number of public sector ones.

Balochistan's share in the Indus river system is an important water source. The province does not form part of the Indus Basin, but is linked to it at Sukkur and Kashmore in Sindh. Hence, Balochistan in a way depends on Sindh for accessing the Indus System waters.

Over-exploitation of groundwater has resulted in its fast depletion. In certain areas, groundwater level is falling at a rate of 10 feet per year and in some places bore wells' depth exceeds 1,000 feet.

The province has no major water storage facilities, except for the Hub dam which was built primarily to ensure water supply to Karachi. During General Musharraf's regime in 2001, two major projects – the Kacchi canal and the Mirani dam – were approved. These projects, currently under implementation, represent the federal government's first water-related initiative after the Hub dam project in the 1960s.

Thus, though agriculture has been the backbone of Balochistan's economy, it is rather hunched from neglect and underdevelopment. There exists no common agriculture policy to integrate the fragmented agricultural activities or to provide impetus to the sector. Worse, the farmers in Balochistan suffer from double taxation – a tax imposed by the provincial government and a 'tax' due to the tribal *Sardar*. This leaves very little re-investible surplus with the farmers. The pathos caused by scarcity of water and of initiative in creating water management systems has only dried up prospects of the agriculture sector. In summary, agriculture in Balochistan is not only a neglected sector, but is also crumbling under the weight of immutable orthodoxy.

Industry

Balochistan has very little to show in terms of industrialisation. There are hardly 200-250 industrial units in Balochistan. Most of the industries are either agro-based or small industries engaged in handicraft, leather and embroidery. Industrial units are concentrated in a few pockets in the Quetta, Nasirabad and Kalat divisions. A large number is located in Lasbela district, in proximity to Karachi.

Balochistan's industry also suffers from gross neglect in the absence of a good industrial policy and enabling infrastructure. The vast mineral resources in the region could have easily engendered a prosperous metal industry. Evidently, successive provincial government's have been apathetic to Balochistan's development. The onus for this morass lies squarely on the federal government. The autonomy available with the provincial government is too little to even chart a meaningful roadmap for development.

The situation has reached a stage where the local populace is no longer willing to accommodate any foreign intervention. The tribal and political pressures exerted on entrepreneurs' strangles the industrial potential.

Minerals

Balochistan is internationally recognised for its rich mineral resources, albeit much remains untapped. Coal, copper, gold, marble, zinc, lead, iron, limestone and other minerals abound.

The Saindak Copper-Gold Project, for which a formal contract between China and Pakistan was signed in September 2003, on coming into full production, will yield an average of 15,810 tonnes of blister copper, 1.5 tonnes of gold and 2.8 tonnes of silver annually for 19 years. The Chinese company will pay $6 million annually to Pakistan over the next 10 years plus 50 per cent of the total revenue from mineral sale. Balochistan will receive $0.7 million per year in royalty.

While the Zhob valley deposits of chromites are well known producing about 20,000 tonnes annually, several iron deposits have also been found in the Chagai district, which has earned the sobriquet "mineral museum" due to the sheer diversity and abundance of minerals found. A number of lead and zinc deposits have been discovered in Lasbela and Khuzdar districts in Balochistan.

Along with metals, Balochistan is gifted with a wide variety of non-metallic elements like coal, gypsum, and barite, to name a few. These minerals are used mostly for domestic consumption although there is a huge potential for export.

Balochistan is well endowed in energy resources like coal and gas. The province has five coalfields with total estimated reserves of 195 million tonnes. It also has deposits of gas hydrates in the form of ice crystalline methane. The province is also estimated to have over 27 trillion cubic feet of recoverable gas reserves. Balochistan is home to one of the largest gas reservoirs in the country, the Sui Gas in Dera Bugti district. Although Balochistan accounts for 41 per cent of the country's total gas production, the province's consumption is only 17 per cent of its total production. It sells 80 per cent of its produce to mainly Punjab and remaining to Sindh. Since Sindh itself has abundant reserves of gas, it does not heavily depend on Balochistan on this count.

The minerals sector is crucial to the development of important economic segments – principally energy, metallurgy and construction. By spawning value-added and downstream segments, employment opportunities can be created. Balochistan's mineral sector is greatly underdeveloped and, in a sense, this explains the overall economic sluggishness. Principal impediments to the province's mineral sector development are:

- Lack of consistent government policy towards mining and metals
- The growth-impinging tribal *Sardari* system
- Inadequate infrastructure and storage handling facilities.

The tribal leaders in the province are known to hinder the efforts of enterprises that have ventured to tap Balochistan's resources. The tribal leaders, if not consulted and made privy to such schemes, are known to scuttle entrepreneurship under the guise of safeguarding their fiefdom. These tribal chiefs are known to demand substantial share from the investors to permit exploration of resources within their territorial domain.

The World Bank, in its study on Pakistan's gas reserves, had asked the federal government to negotiate a new revenue-sharing agreement between tribal leaders, local population and oil companies, to conduct petroleum exploration and production activities, without law and order problems. In this regard, the government offered four major incentives to the people of Balochistan:

Table 4.3: Natural Gas Demand-Supply Position

(million cu mtrs)

	Production	Imports	Exports	Consumption
Punjab	70,227	302,867	-	373,094
Sindh	479,370	-	113,400	365,970
Balochistan	374,161	-	312,023	62,138
NWFP	-	23,402	-	23,402

Source: Pakistan Energy Year Book, 2002

- One-time signature bonus at the time of signing of the agreement with *Sardars* and landowners
- Up to 2.5 per cent royalty to landowners and *Sardars* out of the 12.5 per cent royalty collected by the provincial government
- Production bonus at the rate of $0.5 million to *Sardars*/ landowners payable at the time of commercial production in accordance with the 1947-97 petroleum policy
- Jobs, civic facilities, schools and hospitals for the local population.

However preposterous it might seem, tribal Sardars are known to receive princely royalty from the provincial exchequer. Akbar Bugti, *Sardar* of the Bugti tribe is known to receive Rs.100 million ($1.75 million) annually as royalty for tapping the Sui Gas fields. Though some tribal factions have permitted exploration of natural resources in their domain, there is a handful of Sardars belonging to the major tribes, condemning the issuance of licenses to foreign exploration companies as exploitation and plundering of Balochistan's natural resources for the benefit of Punjab.

Table 4.4: Major Mineral Reserves in Balochistan

Mineral	Unit	Reserves
Barites	Million tns	30
Coal	Million tns	195
Lead and Zinc	Million tns	23
Sulphur	Tonnes	787,000
Iron	Million tns	273
Copper	Million tns	412
Gold	Tonnes	30
Silver	Tonnes	50

Source: Pakistan Geological Survey and Balochistan.sdnpk.org

Security of these mine areas have always come under scrutiny by foreign investors, as Balochistan has witnessed several instances of these areas coming under direct rocket attacks, setting gas wells ablaze and damaging pipelines. Tribals have antagonized projects by resorting to use of heavy weapons, rather than employing civilized means of dissent. Such truculent reaction has deterred foreign investments, and has given the federal government an added responsibility of maintaining law and order around project sites. In order to weaken tribal autocracy, in late 2003, President Musharraf announced the installing of army camps at strategic locations to safeguard these projects. However, the local tribes have not only rejected the proposition, but also threatened to revolt against the government.

The grievances of tribals, which are addressed later in the chapter, are not limited to merely exploration of natural resources by foreign companies or setting up of manufacturing units/export businesses by ethnic groups outside Balochistan. They have even affected major federal government projects like the Gwadar deep-sea port project, which is witnessing growing dissent, with fears voiced of resources being usurped by other provinces.

Gwadar Deep-sea Port Project

The upcoming Gwadar deep-sea port holds the key to Balochistan's potential economic revolution. The Gwadar Port is strategically located on the opposite end of the Gulf of Oman and the Straits of Hormuz, on the mouth of the Persian Gulf. The port would be fully operational by 2005 and is projected to primarily handle transit trade with the landlocked Central Asian Republics, Afghanistan and western China, bordering Pakistan.

As an accompaniment to the core project, supporting physical infrastructure is also coming up. Along with the port project has been launched several road construction projects like the Makran coastal highway, water projects like Mirani dam, Kachhi canal and the Quetta water supply and sanitation project, export processing zones, industrial zones, international airport, etc. There has also been an initiative to develop road infrastructure between Pakistan and Afghanistan. This would greatly improve employment opportunities for the local population and promote industrialisation apart from putting Balochistan on the international trade map.

Some believe that Gwadar is primarily meant for the Pakistan military/navy, as it sees itself as a larger player in the Gulf, elite to realize the potential of the region. However, people have been deprived, evidently for political reasons. The ethnic stronghold of the region and the rebellious tendencies of the locals have forced every successive government to forsake this vast province. Such an attitude, however expedient it might appear, actually reflects lack of political will to ameliorate living conditions and bring locals into mainstream.

The insurgency movement of 1973-77 saw diverse ethnic groups unify under a common threat. The ability of tribal Sardars to rapidly mobilize fragmented tribals into a formidable armed force was proven beyond doubt. From this, Pakistan's polity has learnt to forestall any development that might instigate such unification, and keep Balochistan as disaggregated as possible.

This policy prevails till today.

Political Management of Balochistan

The Baloch community the smallest of population in the country, is the most alienated from capital city Islamabad. The psychological alienation is strongly evident in the recent incidents of sabotage of national assets. Only the Baloch tribes have waged remarkable armed insurgencies against the Pakistani government, and have the capability to repeat it. They have no hopes of gaining significant power in Pakistani politics and are the most receptive to secessionist appeals.

The 1973-77 insurgency aroused unprecedented political awareness among the local Balochis. Perceived discrimination against them in government services and allocation of development funds, settlement of other ethnic groups has led to a sense of deprivation and political disenchantment. Evidence of these deep-seated sentiments, fuelled to a great extent by economic grievances, seems to be resurfacing.

Under present circumstances, another insurgency seems inevitable. A combination of three factors can possibly lead to such a situation: economic deprivation, lack of political space and a channel of expression. The first two factors are already apparent in the province. However, the channel in the form of a unified political platform seems distant.

During the period of insurgency, the regional parties of Baloch tribals were unified on a strong platform, the National Awami Party (NAP), which won the elections in 1970 and formed the first government in collusion with JUI. Sardar Ataullah Mengal headed the coalition government. Apparently, at the time when the NAP formed the government in Balochistan, out of twenty provincial department heads, only one was headed by a Balochi while the remaining were dominated by Punjabis or others. This factor made the nationalists believe that Balochis were being treated as a colony. Added to this, the newly formed government was instructed by the centre to ensure the proper running of the Sui gas plant, which was mostly benefiting Punjab. A third factor alluded to by some writers was geopolitics. The Shah of Iran had expressed his displeasure towards the installing of an NAP government, which was a purely regional party, in the province, lest it gives rise to nationalist tendencies in Iranian Balochistan.

Yet, the NAP-JUI government was formed in Balochistan in 1972 with Ghaus Bux Bizenjo as the first governor and Sardar Ataullah Mengal as the first chief minister of the province. Very soon, in February 1973, Presidential rule was imposed and the NAP-JUI government was dismissed on charges of being involved in an Iraqi consulate arms smuggling scandal.

The Balochi tribals, led by Khair Bux Marri, leader of the Marri tribe, and Sardar Ataullah Mengal, leader of the Mengal tribe, rose in revolt demanding autonomy for the province.

The NAP was banned, following which nationalist forces within the party were left scattered. Members began forming separate parties – Mir Ghaus Bux Bizenjo founded the Pakistan National Party (PNP), Sher Baz Mazari formed the National Democratic Party, Wali Khan and other like-minded elements formed the Awami National Party (ANP).

After the insurgency ended in 1977, two prominent leaders Sardar Ataullah Mengal and Nawab Khair Baksh Marri went on self-exile. In spite of the absence of these leaders, who were in the forefront in organising the revolt, the Baloch youth kept alive the inspiration and formed forums such as the Balochistan National Youth Movement (BNYM). This forum was a component of the Balochistan National Alliance formed by Nawab Akbar Bugti before the 1988 elections. Later, the BNYM was converted into a political party called the Balochistan National Movement. Shortly, the BNM split into two factions: BNM of Dr.Abdul Hye Baloch and the BNM of Sardar Akhtar Mengal, son of Sardar Ataullah Mengal. The PNP also split into three groups.

In August 1990, Nawab Akbar Bugti formed the Jamhoori Watan Party (JWP), which is the only party to make efforts to extend its scope beyond Balochistan to other provinces. There are some Baloch parties that have a presence in NWFP like the BNM and Balochistan National Party.

Thus, following the disbandment of NAP, the nationalist forces in Balochistan kept fragmenting. Except for Nawab Bugti of JWP and some others, all other leaders reduced the scope of their politics to small ethnic groups and tribes. However, reportedly, in recent years, this nationalism has given rise to politicisation of tribal culture. Political parties such as the Hazara Progressive Forum, Kakar Jamhoori Party, Jamote Quami Movement and Barrech Quami Movement, have been formed, all representing their respective tribes.

Balochistan's polity today is highly fragmented and continues to split further, with Nawabs and Sardars heading different parties in pursuit of their respective agenda. Apart from the major tribes that reigned in the past, today several smaller ethnic groups are vying for power in Balochistan's political space.

The conspicuous absence of a strong leadership in Balochistan's politics has left the regional parties at the political periphery. Taking advantage of this leadership deficiency, General Musharraf during the elections in 2002, pre-empted all the regional parties of Balochistan from becoming part of the governing body, by issuing a single decree of minimum graduation as an eligibility clause for contesting the elections. As a result, about 80 per cent of the regional parties were disqualified, and the political space was taken over by national groups, the PML (Q) and Muttahida Majlis-e-Amal (a religious coalition consisting of Pashtuns).

Though MMA does not have any deep affiliation with the local Balochi-ethnic tribes, the Pashtun population in the northern parts of the province played a crucial role in bringing it to power. MMA's coming to power paved way for some drastic revision within Balochistan. Apart from the deep-rooted tribal culture, the MMA is pursuing an agenda of imposing Islamic Sharia in the province. Though not in majority, it has still managed to gain roots. MMA currently holds 16 important portfolios in the provincial cabinet of 31 posts.

Apart from Islamisation, MMA's win has offered the Taliban and Al Qaeda a safe shelter. 9/11 changed the appearance of Balochistan – bringing it into focus for harbouring Al Qaeda and Taliban members. Its proximity to war-torn Afghanistan has caused an influx of refugees and terrorists. This has resulted in tensions along the border areas and in the capital city, Quetta. Year 2003 witnessed the highest number of bomb blast incidents in the capital. Between June and December 2003, there were at least 15 bomb blast incidents in the capital, with frequent reports of rocket attacks and landmine blasts.

Apparently, several Taliban fighters have been taking shelter in mosques and *deeni madaris* in Quetta and surrounding areas since when the war on terror began in Afghanistan. These refugees were receiving complete support from a constituent of MMA, the JUI. One such case is the presence of the notorious Taliban Corp Commander, Mullah Dadullah, spotted in a village near Quetta, who is believed to have allied with the JUI and the Al Qaeda. Mullah Dadullah is responsible for the widely condemned Bamiyan destruction and for several massacres. Also, the Afghan interim President, Hamid Karzai, had termed the Shaldara madrassa in Quetta, run by JUI leader Maulana Nur Mohammed, as the Taliban headquarter.

By making possible the win of a religious party, General Musharraf has indirectly managed to resurrect the Taliban in Balochistan.

Added to the radicalisation of Balochistan society, apparently there has been a record increase in opium cultivation in Balochistan during 2002-2003. According to figures provided by the Pakistan government to the UNDCP, around 2,000 hectares of land has been brought under cultivation of this narcotic.

At present, the fragmented polity of Balochistan does not provide the right milieu for another revolt in the immediate future. However, a rebellion is slowly emerging individually from various Balochi-ethnic groups, visible through incidents of sabotage. In case these tribes are mobilised and channelized to form a unified platform, this can pose a potential threat to Pakistan. The Balochi-ethnic groups in the province are already feeling discriminated in the various development projects undertaken by the federal government. Apart from this, the setting up of army camps in their areas has also irked the locals. In fact, the recent spate of law and order problems within Balochistan and the subsequent decision to set up army camps is viewed as a prelude to another military operation against rebel forces.

The local Balochi-tribes are accustomed to indirect rule, which has given the local *Sardars* considerable measure of autonomy. Though there is no immediate threat of an insurgency in Balochistan, if the federal government decides to impose its hegemony and disrupts the present set up without due consensus, it is bound to unite the Baloch-ethnic groups against the federal government once again. As such, the recent bomb blasts in Quetta and targeting of national assets is a sign of unrest. Already, Sardar Ataullah Mengal who was on self-exile and is well known for his role in 1973 has returned to the country in 2003 and is actively mobilising the regional groups on a single platform. Reportedly, Sardar Khair Bux Marri, who was leading a quite life, has also become active. These incidents are signalling towards another possible uprising, however not immediate.

In fact, the federal government is caught in a Catch-22 situation – if the centre decides to retain Balochistan in its present form, the *Sardars* will continue to rule and the tribal areas will remain active hubs for criminal activities and terrorism. If the government decides to penetrate these regions by force through development projects and other socio-economic changes, which seems likely, it is bound to irk the tribesmen who have no qualms in taking to arms and revolt. The federal government will therefore have to face one more confrontation with the locals before effecting any major transformation in the region.

Also a very potent threat emerging in recent times is the possible unification of Balochis residing in Pakistan, Iran and Afghanistan. Though in a nascent stage, the educated Balochi youth in these countries are actively considering the concept of a Greater Balochistan.

Prospects

Growth

Balochistan has the potential to emerge as a major trade hub of the country, apart from a rich source of mineral wealth. Its importance is bound to rise even for international traffic, acting as a conduit to Central Asian countries. This can have a manifold impact on the economy of Balochistan.

However, Balochistan's primary problem is paucity of human resources and capital, tribal traditions and ineffective policies. Its youth, hardly educated to make any significant contribution to the economy, is a deprived lot relegated to doing menial jobs.

The province is caught in an economic impasse – it does not generate enough financial resources to break the jinx of underdevelopment and will remain trapped till the federal government decides to pump in resources to transform the economy. However, Pakistan has followed a policy of promoting the agriculture sector and related industries, rather than capital goods industries, which has left Balochistan out of its scope. Balochistan's agricultural potential is constrained by infertile land and severe drought. Whenever the drought recedes, Balochistan can rely on horticulture, producing quality fruits targeting overseas markets.

Balochistan can potentially excel in mining and mineral-based industries. Lately Pakistan's policy makers have been focussing towards development of the mineral sector through international assistance. Investments have been sought in the mining sector, and several foreign companies are already operating in the province. This would improve Balochistan's standing.

The tribal dispensation of the province is the root of underdevelopment. Traditions restrict social interactions, forcing tribes to behave as autonomous units within a larger state. Government efforts to attract foreign investments are often scuttled by the local chiefs if they are not given due monetary compensation. They put forward list of unreasonable demands, which often end up making the project unviable. Moreover, these tribes are unwilling to accommodate ethnic groups from outside the province, which only complicates matters.

This situation has forced the federal government to impose its demands on the province, rather than take consensus. Such forceful penetration of the region could aggravate law and order problems and prepare ground for another confrontation with the centre.

Balochistan will have to depend on federal government funding and external resources to generate employment. So long as its local leader, Mir Zafarullah Khan Jamali continues as Prime Minister of Pakistan, Balochistan can hope to receive some fiscal relief. However, foremost, the local tribal leaders will have to be taken into confidence and assured of due compensation to their tribesmen in every project undertaken. Further, it is utmost essential to bring about a gradual socio-economic transformation of the province to reap any substantial benefit. Although foreign investors are willing to invest in Balochistan, they will not come till the socio-economic situation improves and law and order stabilizes.

The commissioning of the Gwadar port would transform Balochistan's prospects from 2005. It would not only expand Balochistan's realm of economic activities but also place it on the international trade map. Further, if the province were able to attract investments in the mineral sector for exploration and setting up of downstream industries, this would greatly enhance not only its economic output, but would also propel social development. The revenue earned through direct transfers from the federal government, in the form of royalty, would help in bringing much-needed funds for local development. However, much of this vision would be possible only if the local population is pervious to the forces of transformation.

Today, with no unity of purpose among the various factions, prospects of economic development look bleak in Balochistan.

Governance and God

Tribalism is a deep-rooted reality of Balochistan. Society is structured on traditional lines, which has by far kept the people of the province alienated from the progressive and technologically advanced world. Land and water are considered prime assets, and form the bases of violent inter-tribe conflicts. Despite Balochistan's traditional backwardness, weapons are dangerously commonplace, reflecting the innate Balochi tendency to revolt rather than reform. Some have learnt the skills of weapons making, and constant violent confrontations has kept the province under perennial law and order problems.

Added to this, the win of Muttahida Majlis-e-Amal, which has explicitly expressed its desire to bring in Islamisation, has impelled the province towards further radicalization. The ruling party, which holds several important portfolios in the present cabinet, has already drafted a Shariat Bill for the province.

MMA's success of installing Islamic governance in the province can have far reaching implications. Tribalism along with Islamic mode of governance will put the province on the path to backwardness. If governance promotes religious zealots, it would lead to an increase in conservatism, violence, abuse and discrimination against women, and the arms and drug culture. Investment would be deterred, further alienating the province from Islamabad. The region would become impregnable and a haven for nefarious activities and terrorism.

Tribalism along with Islamisation can prove a deadly combination in engendering radical Islam. So far, however, the influence of MMA has remained restricted to the northern Pashtun-dominated areas of the province. It is difficult for orthodox Islam to take roots in the southern parts of the province, which is the stronghold of Balochi-ethnic tribals. These tribesmen are staunch followers of tribal traditions, which extend beyond the constitution and courts.

Thus, radical Islam will essentially remain a political process, brought in by the MMA. However, this can possibly lead to an ethnic conflict between the Balochi and the Pasthun population.

A clash between the various ethnic factions will once again prompt the army to intervene and this time to establish a permanent presence. The army is already finding it difficult to penetrate the region without irking the tribal leaders, who instantly take to arms. An ethnic clash in the province will provide the army legitimacy to intervene extensively.

Besides ethnic polarization, Balochistan may also witness split between religious extremism and nationalism. These tendencies are represented by the Pashtun-dominated MMA and Sardar-dominated tribal groups, respectively. Sardar Ataullah Mengal's return to Pakistan and actions of other tribal leaders can galvanize Balochi nationalism. So long as religious extremism and Balochi nationalism have common interests to unite against the federal leadership, they will collaborate. Eventually, they are bound to seek to expand their respective space. This will set in motion a dangerous competition and with both sides armed, it can also lead to a violent confrontation.

As there is a tacit alliance between the military and mullahs, the army will support religious extremists. This may force the nationalists to seek a separate identity. The unfinished agenda of 1973 may be sought to be finished, which by present trends will occur around in 2007.

Geopolitics

The commissioning of the Gwadar port would bring Balochistan into international limelight, especially as a conduit to Central Asian Republics (CARs). The port is coming up through Chinese assistance. China perceives the region as a feasible route to access the oil rich CARs. Further, China has invested in mineral projects in Balochistan, and the port would facilitate easy transportation.

The US perceives China as its main strategic competitor by 2020 in the Asia-Pacific theatre. It would like to develop relations with other countries in Asia to counter China's potential challenge to US supremacy. As a means to this end, it would want to have an influence in the foreign policy and national security apparatus of Pakistan.

China wants close relations with Pakistan for economic reasons. It would want to develop Pakistan as a dependable supplier of energy and minerals, which explains China's keenness to develop Pakistan's infrastructure, especially the Gwadar port, railways, roads and mineral resources. China has already planned extensive commercial relations with Pakistan for the next ten years.

US will try to deter this close bonding, and Balochistan, in the bargain, will become the centre for interplay of international forces. The US, in its bid to have a presence in the region, is planning a naval base in the region adjacent to Gwadar.

In the short run, China will accept US presence in the region, complying with its policy of non-confrontation with the US, at least till 2010. The Chinese would be willing to negotiate stability with the US in return for the latter's soft attitude towards Taiwan. The Chinese are willing to give the US a free hand to operate in Central Asia, Afghanistan and also in Pakistan.

A second factor for Chinese acquiescence to the US is the war against terrorism, to which China has also pledged its support, because of its own issues of terrorism in Xinjiang province in northern China. So long as terrorism in Xinjiang continues, China will cooperate. Until 2010, no confrontation is expected.

Beyond 2010, if Chinese economic drive is successful, then by 2015 China would contribute 30-40 per cent of the global manufacturing output. By this time, they would have resolved the Xinjiang issue as well. Their top priority would then shift towards ensuring energy supplies. At this stage Gwadar will become important. China is already tapping the Central Asian markets, and has invested in Kazakhstan. Pakistan has also entered into transit trade agreements with Kazakhstan, and is planning similar agreements with the other countries.

This will lead to a conflict of interests between US and China, which will be staged in Balochistan. US's interest in the region is twofold – security and energy – while the Chinese interests in purely to ensure energy supplies. Both the countries will try to control factions within the Pakistani army in order to realize their specific interests.

To get *de facto* control, US and China may even directly support certain local groups, if need be. If there is secession, both China and US will wrest for control over the region.

However, Balochistan's economic importance largely hinges on the stability in Afghanistan – the channel to access CAR's. If Afghanistan does not attain stability, then Gwadar port would lose its efficacy.

Iran is also a stakeholder in this battle. The coming up of Gwadar port would affect the traffic at Iran's Chabahar port, which is also being promoted as a conduit to CARs. Once development catches up in Balochistan, the Sistan-Balochestan region of Iran may come under threat and could rise in revolt against the Iranian government.

The situation in Afghanistan will also have a bearing on Balochistan's future. If Afghanistan disintegrates, the Baloch population of Afghanistan may decide to migrate to the fast expanding Balochistan in Pakistan. Alternatively, the Balochi people of Afghanistan and Pakistan may seek to form a new Republic of Balochistan.

Forecast

Area around Gwadar will develop leading to industrialisation, infrastructure development, exports, etc. It would have a positive impact on employment prospects. However, the negative implications include economic dislocation of local population and influx of labour from other provinces

Trend

1) If Jamali continues in power, fiscal allocations will steadily increase for Balochistan, thus further contributing to development in the region
2) MMA influence will increase due to significant Pashtun population in the northern areas and fluidity in Afghanistan.

Discontinuity

1) General Musharraf's social engineering will dismantle the present tribal structure. However, his exit will terminate the efforts.
2) Success of the movement led by Ataullah Mengal will strengthen separatist tendencies.
3) Failure of Karzai government and Afghanistan's return to chaos will render Gwadar port less efficacious.
4) A conflict between religious extremism and Balochi nationalism will generate ideological and ethnic polarization.

Wild Card

1) Agitation in Sindh reaches an extreme stage, this will spill into Balochistan leading to fragmentation of Pakistan.
2) In case of fragmentation of Pakistan or chaos at the centre, US and China will struggle to gain control over Gwadar region.
3) The Balochis of Afghanistan and Pakistan seek an independent Balochistan.

CHAPTER 5

North West Frontier Province

North West Frontier Province (NWFP), also known as *Sarhad*, is the smallest province in Pakistan. It is spread over an area of 101,471 sq km. Located on both banks of the River Indus; the province stretches from the Himalayas in the north and borders Punjab and Balochistan in the south, Afghanistan lies on the west of NWFP and Kashmir (Pakistan) on its east. The administrative structure of the province consists of 7 divisions and 24 districts. To date, it retains the British tradition of being divided into settled districts and tribal agencies. The settled area, covering 74,251 sq km, is governed by the provincial government with the governor as head. The administrative structure is only limited to the settled areas. The tribal agencies, known as Federally Administered Tribal Areas (FATA), are administered by political officers who directly report to the federal government.

NWFP's location has been historically important as a point of entry for several famous conquerors and adventurers to the sub-continent, which include Mahmood of Ghazni, Alexander the Great, Taimur, Emperor Babar, Nadir Shah and Ahmed Shah Abdali. The Khyber Pass has been a vital route between Pakistan and Afghanistan. The Pashtun tribe, the dominant ethnic group in the province, is spread up to Afghanistan's eastern parts.

FATA lies to the west of the provincial capital Peshawar spread up to the borders with Afghanistan. The British could never control the tribal area during its rule, and Pakistan government never penetrated the region, barring entry to civilians and military, till the day the War on Terror began.

In 1893, the then British government succeeded in drawing the imaginary Durand Line marking the boundaries between Pakistan and Afghanistan, which cut through the Pashtun-dominated tribal areas. However, the fierce Pashtun tribe rebuffed the international boundary and the borders remained porous. Due to the strong ethnic linkages on both sides of the border, it proved difficult to keep these tribes confined within the national boundary. This close link has time and again excited the Pashtunistan movement, which Pakistan has frenetically tried to suppress. Moreover, Afghanistan has also maintained an ambivalent posture, occasionally raising doubts regarding the status of the Durand Line with Pakistan, thus covertly exposing its interests in the Pashtun-dominated areas of Pakistan.

On the Pashtun issue, relations between Pakistan and Afghanistan have remained bitter since the 1950s. Pakistan has tried hard to suppress the Pashtunistan issue by accommodating the ethnic group in the country's military-bureaucratic-economic structure. The maintenance of status quo of the tribal areas, even after the British withdrew, proved a significant move in negating any possible separatist effort. However, in recent times, the borders have come under special focus, as Taliban (who belong to the Pashtun clan) and Al Qaeda members are believed to be finding shelter in the autonomous tribal regions. Military operations in these regions, along with the involvement of the US military, became inevitable much to the consternation of the local tribesmen.

Ever since the war on terror began in Afghanistan, the status of the Durand Line as a boundary has come under cloud. In 2003-2004, a major part of the war was being fought along the borders, with the tribals in the region coming under direct attacks from both sides – from the US coalition troops on the Afghan side and the Pakistani army on its side. Amidst these operations, there were reports of the Afghan government restoring incentives for tribesmen, including those on the Pakistani side. The Afghan militia was distributing salaries to tribesmen living in South Waziristhan Agency in FATA – evidently a move to buy their loyalty and support.

The autonomous status of the tribal region has since been nullified. The Pakistani military has undertaken several development projects on a war footing in the region, especially the building of roads and communication network to improve accessibility. Several development projects, like setting up of water retention facilities, schools, hospitals, etc have also been initiated expeditiously.

Since, the fusion of Pashtuns into Pakistan's mainstream, the Pashtunistan is more or less resolved, except in the tribal areas. The issue has transmuted into a demand for provincial autonomy. However, the tragedy of 1971 has been so overpowering on Islamabad, that any demand for autonomy is perceived with apprehension. Demand for renaming the NWFP to Pakhtunkhwa or Pakhtoonistan is also being rejected by the Pakistan government, as it fears that any name closely linked with ethnic and language identity can instigate a sub-nationalist movement. As for the progress of tribal areas, where the factors affecting the Pashtun issue are non-economic and unrelated to Punjab, the relationship of Islamabad with Afghanistan and a solution to the Afghan crisis, would be a determining factor.

The province has historically been an important trade route to Central Asia, albeit through land routes via Afghanistan. The distance from here to the European markets is much shorter than from Karachi. This proximity and locational advantage can offer great scope provided the FATA areas become accessible and the Afghan situation stabilises. Till then, the region is bound to suffer economically.

Population

The population of NWFP increased from about 8 million in 1972 to approximately 18 million in 1998. It had the highest population growth rateof 2.75 per cent in the country. In 2003, population had already touched 20 million, and by the end of the decade, It is likely to cross 25 million. A large part of the increase can be attributed to the presence of Afghan refugees who have managed to blend with the local population and even enter the economic mainstream.

According to the government of Pakistan, there were about 3-4 million displaced Afghan refugees living in Pakistan in 2003. Of these, most of them reside in NWFP with a marked presence in the capital city Peshawar. Many of these Afghans have acquired Pakistani citizenship. The presence of a large Afghan population in NWFP is a matter of concern, more so because they seem to have gained acceptance by the locals, in view of the strong ethnic communalities.

Nearly three-fourth of NWFP's population comprises of

Pashtuns, whose society comprises settled as well as the tribal areas. The Pashtuns in the settled areas have been exposed to external influence and hence practise tempered traditional values. However, the Pashtuns living in the tribal belt have abided by the true Pashto ethos. Traditionally, the conduct of Pashtun is guided by a code of conduct called the Pukhtunwali, that advocates taking revenge for wrong done but hospitality towards a guest, stranger or an enemy if its sought. Pashtuns are divided into several tribes like the Yousufzai, Muhammadzai, Khalil who belong mostly to the settled districts, and others like Afridi, Waziri, Banauchi, and Orakzai to name a few, who are extensively spread in the settled as well as the tribal areas.

Only 17 per cent of NWFP, excluding the tribal areas, is urbanized, with a concentration in the central parts of the province, around Peshawar. Five out of 23 districts in the province – Peshawar, Nowshera, Charsadda, Mardan and Kohat – are developed. Population density in these districts is consequently high. Peshawar has a population density of 1,600 people per sq km, followed by Charsadda with 1,027, Mardan with 895 and Nowshera with 500. The five districts are also the most important in terms of industrialisation and as preferred destinations for new investments. The remaining parts of the province, especially the southern and northern parts are least developed. The Chitral and Kohistan districts, both located in the northern part of the province, are the least populous.

The population profile of NWFP, as per the Census of 1998, suggests high concentration of youth. Nearly 58 per cent of the population is within the age group of 19 years. Youth population in the age group of 15-24 comprises 19 per cent of the total population. This implies that NWFP has a daunting task of gearing up to an explosion in its workforce in years to come. In the current decade, five million people, or 31 per cent of the population, are likely to join the workforce.

Overall literacy levels are an uninspiring 37 per cent as per the Census of 1998. However, this metric is a statistical aberration as it reflects the poor literacy levels among the older population. In the youth population (age group of 15-24), the literacy rate is 48 per cent.

Interestingly, while male literacy in the province has reached 53 per cent (72 per cent urban and 48 per cent rural), female literacy barely touches 21 per cent (43 per cent urban, 17 per cent rural). This disparity reflects the extant social structure where female education is not encouraged. Informal education, in the form of religious schools popularly known as madrassas, is very common in the province and these schools mostly provide education to boys.

The settled areas of NWFP are headed for a major transformation in the near future. The youth population is educated and can prove a major asset if wisely channelized. Providing employment opportunities to these youngsters is crucial, lest unemployment leads them to fundamentalism. However, much hinges on the form of governance adopted in the province. The present government of Muttahida Majlis-e-Amal (MMA), a religious coalition, can either convert the region into a prosperous economic hub or a fundamentalist state by promoting rigid Islamic laws. Adopting of the *Sharia* by the provincial government has been a step towards religious indoctrination and reinforcement of the rule of the clerics. So far, however, implementation of the religious system has been half-hearted. Economic policy-making has been execrable.

Table 5.1: NWFP's Ethnic Composition

(% share)

Area	Urdu	Punjabi	Sindhi	Pushto	Balochi	Seraiki	Others
Total	0.8	1.0	-	73.9	-	3.9	20.4
Rural	0.3	0.2	-	74.0	-	4.0	21.5
Urban	0.5	4.6	-	73.5	-	3.2	15.1

The proximity to war-torn Afghanistan and their ethnic homogeneity can have a widespread impact on NWFP society. Furthermore, the presence of millions of Afghan refugees, who are willing to work at sub-normal wages, pushing local Pashtuns to unemployment, which portends social strife.

Economy

Till the 1970s, NWFP's contribution to the national economy was trifling. In 1969-70, the province's share in Pakistan's GDP was barely 8 per cent. After the Soviet invasion of Afghanistan in 1979, Pakistan received large amounts of foreign aid. NWFP was a major recipient with much of the monies spent on basic infrastructure development. Foreign NGOs donated billions of dollars for rehabilitation of Afghan refugees. Rich amongst those who migrated from war-torn Afghanistan into NWFP, brought in large sums of money, that was invested in Peshawar and neighbouring areas. An unhealthy accompaniment of the Afghan war was the migration of the smuggling, narcotics and arms culture into NWFP. This created an elite class of parvenu warlords. Perhaps the most important factor was the large number of NWFP migrants to the Gulf States and the subsequent inflow of foreign remittances. This changed the socio-economic situation in the province.

Inward remittances spirited up the province's economy in the 1980s. However, the economy suffered during the 1990s, when aid money dried up and remittances slowed down. Added to this, drought worsened the agricultural situation in the province and industry suffered. According to the Sarhad Chamber of Commerce and Industry, nearly 40 per cent of industries in the NWFP have closed down, since the 1990s.

Nevertheless, post 9/11 and the MMA's return to power has once again brought this region into international focus. If nothing else, the international community would pump in funds to counter the threat of fundamentalism and protect the social, economic and political structure against destruction. It cannot let Pakistan go the Afghanistan way – considering nuclear weapons and strategic interest – and will try to actuate social development, despite the MMA.

Today, NWFP's contribution to the national economy has touched 13 per cent. Though a 5-percentage point increase since 1970, it is scant progress compared to the inflow of funds that the province received over the past two decades. The Social Policy and Development Centre, in its annual review of 2000, stated that during 1996-97, NWFP received Rs.16.2 billion in the form of remittances – 23 per cent of total remittances in the country. A comparable parameter could be the Annual Development Plan of NWFP, which stood at a lower Rs.13 billion in 2002-03.

Superficially, NWFP seems the fastest growing economy in the country in terms of per capita income. However, the province's meagre contribution to the country's GDP is an indication that the economy of NWFP is more dependent on remittances and the vacillating services sector. Easy inflow of funds has given rise to consumerism rather than capital formation.

NWFP is primarily an agrarian economy, contending with the mountainous terrain that does not favour extensive cultivation. Tobacco and maize are major produce. Export of tobacco is an important revenue source. Hydro electricity generation is another significant economic activity contributing to the exchequer. NWFP is well endowed with mineral resources. Apart from these, tourism also has tremendous potential, but has received a major setback since the war in Afghanistan.

The province has an under-developed industrial base with incipient signs of progress. Small-scale industries, mainly in areas of furniture making and handicrafts, play an important role.

According to estimates presented by the Social Policy and Development Centre, NWFP had the lowest incidence of income poverty in the country of 23 per cent in 1996-97. Per capita income grew at a rate of 2.9 per cent annually from 1980 to 1999. Income prosperity is comfortable. However, income poverty is just one aspect, and in terms of social deprivation and development, implied poverty is higher in the province.

Out of 24 districts, nine are reasonably developed while 15 are in the low development category. Peshawar is the hub of economic activity in the province. The Peshawar-Nowshehra-Mardan-Charsadda region, though belonging to heterogeneous administrative districts, is the most developed belt in the province. Together, these four districts, all within a small radius from Peshawar contain 30 per cent of NWFP's total population. Any plan to develop Peshawar will hinge on this belt.

According to the HIES 2001-02, NWFP has 2.2 million households with an average size of 8 persons per household. Over 56 per cent of the houses are concrete structures. In terms of household amenities, 72 per cent of households have electricity connection. However, only 10 per cent of them receive gas supplies and 39 per cent have tap water connection. Electrification has been possible due to the abundant hydro-electricity generation in the province, but other household amenities are lacking.

The domestic economy of NWFP provides limited opportunities and subsidiary existence to its population. Agriculture is the primary activity in the province as per official statistics. However, many earn their living in trade activities, especially transit trade through Afghanistan. Import of goods from Afghanistan without paying custom and other taxes is a major source of income for Pashtuns. It also supports other activities like transport, unorganised entrepreneurship and real estate in NWFP. At present, only four items – television sets, telephones, tyres & tubes and motor spare parts – remain in the negative list for Pak-Afghan transit trade. In 2002-03, the total value of Afghan Transit Trade had touched Rs.16.4 billion.

Significant transfer of funds from expatriates keeps demand levels high. Exports of rugs and precious stones also rake in substantial foreign exchange earnings. Donations and support from Arabs also add to income generation. These funds are mostly channelled to *deeni madaris* in the province to promote the Wahabi school of thought. Iran also provides funds for supporting Shi'a followers. NWFP is also a playground for international competition between Saudi Arabia and Iran, both vying to control NWFP's social machinery.

However, not all income earned is legal. Drug trafficking, smuggling and sale of arms and weapons are a major source of foreign exchange. Black economy flourishes in NWFP. The main centres for illegal activities in Pakistan include Quetta, Punjab, Karachi and NWFP. Pakistan's total terror-economy is estimated to be of the order Rs.264 billion, of which, at least 30 per cent or Rs.79 billion is generated in NWFP.

Agriculture

NWFP is predominantly an agrarian economy employing over 40 per cent of the working population. NWFP accounts for around 19 per cent of total cultivated area in Pakistan, and only five per cent of total irrigated area. Though a state abundant in water resources, 50 per cent of the land in NWFP is not under irrigation. Irrigation is mostly carried out through underground water resources.

Crops grown include wheat, rice, sugarcane, cotton, tobacco, maize and barley. Wheat has the largest area under cultivation in the province. However, in terms of significant contribution to overall production in the country, tobacco, maize and barley are noteworthy with a share of 75 per cent, 45 per cent and 24 per cent respectively. Tobacco cultivation is spread over just 3 per cent of total cultivated area in NWFP but is a major foreign exchange earner – around Rs.362 million ($6.3 million) in 2002-03. It is also a labour intensive activity involving about 80,000 persons in cultivation, 50,000 in 26 tobacco factories and another one million indirectly employed in trading.

Livestock rearing is another major activity, generating around 70 per cent of rural income. At the provincial level, livestock sector holds a share of 17 per cent in the total value of production. The sector also produces hides and skins and their by-products that contribute to 10 per cent of total export earnings of the country.

Though agriculture is a predominant activity, the sector receives insignificant outlay in the Annual Development Programme of the province. In 2002-03, the province had earmarked hardly seven per cent of its ADP for the agriculture and forestry sector. A major part of the outlay was in fact assigned to the water sector, especially hydropower generation. NWFP contributes 44 per cent to Pakistan's total hydropower generation.

Water Resources in NWFP

NWFP is home to the most important reservoir of Pakistan – the Tarbela dam. The Indus river and many other smaller western tributaries and streams flow through this province. The western rivers are Chitral, Swat, Panjkora, Kabul, Tochi, Kurram and Gomal, all of which have high potential for hydropower generation. Apart from the Tarbela dam, the Warsak dam and Chashma barrage are also located in this province.

Most of the underground and surface water in the province is "sweet", with the exception of brackish water zones in D.I. Khan, Bannu and Karak districts in the southern part of the province. Though the prevailing drought conditions have affected agricultural production in the province to some extent, the province, on the whole, is placed better than the others.

The province has lately been focussing on developing its water resources. It was planning to set up four small dams in districts facing water scarcity. The province has also envisaged 550 water schemes under the Drought Emergency Relief Assistance Programme. Hydro-electricity generation is another arena where the provincial government has been making clear-cut efforts.

NWFP generates 44 per cent of the hydropower produced in Pakistan. Within the province, out of the total energy generation of 19,940.58 GWh in 2003, over 80 per cent came from hydroelectric plants. The province receives around Rs.6 billion from the federal government as its share in hydropower profits. Water resource management in the province would definitely carry nation-wide implications, considering that rest of Pakistan is likely to face serious water shortages by the end of the decade.

Minerals

NWFP is endowed with natural resources and is home to some rare minerals. The mineral map of Pakistan reflects a high concentration of a variety of metallic and non-metallic minerals in the northern parts of the country, mostly in NWFP. The eastern and the central parts of the province such as Cherat, Nowshehra, Peshawar, Swabi, Haripur, Mansehra and Abottabad have the largest concentration of minerals. So far, fifty-three varieties of minerals including coal, oil, gas, marble, granite, phosphate, slatestone, emerald and topaz, have been discovered in the province.

Table 5.2: Mineral Production in NWFP (1999-2000)

(Tonnes)

Minerals	Production
Barites	2,233
China Clay	46,806
Coal	46,355
Gypsum	123,961
Lime Stone	4,305,485
Marble	455,665
Rock Salt	121,092
Silica Sand	26,877
Slate Stone	132,427
Dolomite	174,588
Emerald	3183.25 cts.
Jade	20

Source: Directorate of Industries, Commerce & Mineral Dev (Mineral Wing) Government of NWFP

The NWFP government is planning to allow private sector companies to undertake exploration in specified gemstone deposit areas. Plans are also afoot to set up a Gem Industrial Estate in the province. Gemstones worth Rs.6.56 million were exported from the NWFP during 2002.

Marble is NWFP's most valued natural resource. Vast marble reserves exist in several pockets of the province, and constitute 97 per cent of the country's total 160 million tonnes of proven

Table 5.3: Industries in NWFP in 1999-2000

Industry	Numbers
Flour Mills	75
Silk	66
Plastic & Rubber	43
Textile	40
Engineering	38
Food	36
Furniture & Wood	32
Chemical	27
Metal Work	27
Pharmaceutical	27
Tobacco	27
Marble & Chips	23
Ghee	22
Cement based	24
Appliances	17
Leather & Foot	15
Matches	14
Hosiery	10
Woollen	9
Beverages	8
Others	86
Total	666

Source: NWFP Bureau of Statistics

deposit. The best marble is found in Buner, Swat, Mardan and Nowshera districts and the Malakand agency of NWFP as well as the adjoining Mohmand and Khyber agencies in the FATA. In so far as fuel minerals are concerned, the province recently discovered two gas reserves in the Karat and Kohat districts.

The current MMA government is streamlining the development of natural resources as a base for the province's economic growth, involving foreign and private investment. A case in point is the Toronto International, which set up gold exploration projects in 2001 within 7,500 sq km area in Chitral.

Industry

According to the NWFP Bureau of Statistics, there were 666 industrial units operating in the province in 1999-2000. Food, beverages and tobacco are leading sectors followed by textiles and leather. There are about ten industrial estates, including small ones, which are fully operational. An Export Processing Zone is also established at Risalpur town near Peshawar.

About one-third of NWFP's industrial activity takes place in Peshawar alone. Peshawar's industrial base has a pronounced diversity.

There are numerous flourmills in the province, which dependent on Punjab for wheat supplies. In fact, till the 1970s, Punjab fulfilled a great share of demand for consumer and intermediate goods in NWFP. However, since the mid-1980s, Pashtun industrialists around Mardan, Nowshehra and Peshawar have accelerated local production. An important factor that helped in industrialising the province was the slowdown in Sindh's economy. In fact, Karachi was undergoing de-industrialisation, which led to industrial migration to Punjab and NWFP.

The industrialisation process in NWFP has also witnessed a countervailing force in the form of closures of units. The impending WTO regime is expected to further erode NWFP's industrial sector, with small and unorganised units becoming first victims. It is felt that entrepreneurship in NWFP might shift from manufacturing to trading.

NWFP's limping industrial sector is not likely to pick up in the near future. Industrial development hardly receives any attention as reflected in the Annual Development budget of the province. In 2002-03, the government had allocated just 0.2 per cent of the total outlay for development. Many more industrial units face imminent closure.

Overall, the government is focused towards developing hydropower, minerals and tourism. All these sectors have been opened up to foreign participation, although the investment is only a trickle. The investment climate is still not conducive to foreign investment, thanks to traditional apathetic MMA policies.

NWFP is in a paradoxical situation. The MMA government, adhering to its election manifesto, is foremost working towards bringing in Islamic governance with the passing of the Shariah Act. The more controversial Hasba (Accountability) Bill is being put in place, which aims to set up a parallel judiciary system for the promotion of virtue and prevention of vice. These policies are in sharp contrast to the federal government's own commitments and guidelines. As a result, the centre has been in direct confrontation with the MMA government. This process has effectively kept the provincial government in continuous political bickering with the centre. Since potential foreign investment will have to be routed through the centre,

Table 5.4: Foreign Aid to NWFP

Aid	Major Donors	Sectors
Loans: Rs. 4640.4 Mln	ADB (73%)	Education, Health,
Grants: Rs. 546.1 Mln	World Bank (7%)	Water, Agriculture,
	SDC (4%)	Roads, Forestry and
	Netherlands (3%)	Rural Development
	IFAD (4%)	
	U.N Agencies (1%)	
	Others-GTZ, JICA, CIDA (8%)	

Source: Pakistan Development Forum, 2003 – Government of NWFP

the ongoing federal-provincial tussle is bound to be a roadblock.

The province's dependence on foreign aid and fiscal help from the federal government, would only add to NWFP's despair.

Relations with the Federal Government

NWFP finances at most 10 per cent of its expenditure through internal revenue generation, relying on the federal government to the extent of 90 per cent for its revenue requirements. In the provincial budget of 2003-04, revenue expenditure was estimated at Rs.47.1 billion out of which Rs.3.7 billion was financed from provincial tax receipts. NWFP's contribution to the national exchequer is about 6 per cent.

Till 2002-03, the province had an outstanding federal debt of Rs.74 billion. In fiscal 2002-03, the province received foreign aid to the tune of Rs.4.6 billion in the form of loans and Rs.0.5 billion as grants, implying high dependence on foreign funding.

The entire system of governmental transfers in Pakistan is such that federal debt, and therefore a deficit provincial budget, is inevitable.

This has been one of the reasons for the MMA government's demand for provincial autonomy and also higher share in profits from hydropower generation. The emergence of MMA in two provinces – NWFP and Balochistan – a strong contender for the federal government presages its development into a political powerhouse.

Ever since the MMA took over the mantle of governing NWFP, it has been raising the issue of autonomy at every forum. However, its demand for autonomy is more to camouflage its own deficiencies in economic management. It is being used as a political tool.

Although MMA government presented a laudable maiden budget, focussing on social sector development and fiscal management, it skimped on the implementation of the proposals. The MMA is indeed gaining in stature and reach, but not on the strength of perceptible social development. MMA's omnipresent demand for provincial autonomy, a purely political move, has been masquerading as the government's alternative approach for development.

A major achievement as claimed by the provincial government has been the passage of the Shariah Act on June 2, 2003, and the introduction of interest-free banking – a key step towards establishing a true Islamic society. Also, there has been effort towards setting up medical colleges and a university for women. Outside these, there is no concrete proposal towards capital formation and employment generation.

People of NWFP are growing circumspect of MMA's economic policies. The MMA government does not have any industrial or trade policy. Though it has promised to eradicate poverty and generate employment, no visible effort in this direction is apparent. Lost in their narrow agenda of

- Jamia Saaraf Ul Uloom Tamir Giroh in Lakki Marru, run by Parliamentary leader of MMA, Maulana Gul Naseeb Khan
- Madrassa Darul Uloom Arabia run by MPA Kari Abdulla Bangash from NWFP
- Madrassa Fatah-ul-Uloom in Shahidabad run by MPA Maulana Shah Abdul Aziz
- Madrassa Darul Uloom Islamia, in Charsadda run by Maulana Idrees, MPA
- Markaz Darul Quraa in Peshawar run by MNA Qari Fayaz ul Rehman Alvi
- Madrassa Al Markaz-e-Islami in Bannu, run by Maulana Syed Naseeb Ali Shah
- Jamia Arabia Siddiquia Al Uloom in Peshawar run by MNA Abdul Akbar
- Madrassa Darul Uloom Islamiya Arabia in Mardan led by MNA Maulana Mohd. Qasim
- Jamia Islamia Tafheen-al-Quran in Mardan run by Maulana Gauhar Rehman and his son Dr. Maulana Atta-ur-Rehman who is a MNA.

Though, the federal ministry of education has continuously been trying to persuade the madaris to register themselves, the government, in over a year, has managed to get only 1,200 madaris into its fold.

Federally Administered Tribal Areas (FATA)

Area (sq km)	27,220
Population (numbers)	3,176,000
Urban (%)	2.7
Rural (%)	97.3
Pop Growth Rate (%)	2.19
Pop / Cult.Hec	17
Pop / Irr. Hec	32
Literacy Rate (%)	17
Poverty (%)	60

FATA comprises of seven agencies: Khyber, Kurram, Orakzai, Mohmand, Bajaur, North Waziristan and South Waziristan. These tribal agencies have historical, cultural and ethnic ties with Afghanistan and are inhabited by fiercely independent tribesmen, many of whom share deep sympathies for the Taliban.

The FATA is *de facto* an independent region, outside the control of Islamabad and enjoy considerable geo-political importance. Following their ouster from Afghanistan, most Taliban leaders found sanctuary among fellow ethnic Pashtuns in the tribal regions and Balochistan. As tribesmen controlled these areas with hardly any interference from the Pakistani government, they became safe havens for the Taliban and Al Qaeda.

The economy of FATA is agrarian with most locals engaged in livestock rearing. Besides agriculture, the FATA areas are gifted with mineral resources. However, the tribesmen do not permit external interference, and the minerals remain unexplored.

Since FATA lies in a strategic location, bordering Afghanistan, the Government of Pakistan has realised the need to penetrate these inaccessible regions. For this purpose, several development schemes have been initiated. However, this was a knee-jerk awareness on the part of the Pakistan government following the 9/11 incident. The army decided to undertake development activities in the region, and apparently, by 2002, they managed to build important roads. This has made the region accessible. Also, they revoked the tag of 'No-go' areas thus declaring the region accessible.

The NWFP government also decided to initiate several infrastructure projects like building water retention facilities, roads and undertake industrial development, with an allocation of Rs.3 billion. There has also been a growing emphasis on developing education and health facilities.

In a highly conservative society where women venturing out of their houses, is unheard of, building schools is a rare positive step. With the war on terror having impacted FATA in a big way, due to its proximity to Afghanistan and the presence of Taliban in the region, there is bound to be a major socio-political and economical upheaval in the days to come.

Political Management

Among the three smaller provinces - NWFP, Sindh and Balochistan - NWFP is more closely integrated with Islamabad. NWFP has had a fairly good representation of 13.1 per cent in the federal bureaucracy. A few of the former Presidents of the country have been Pashtuns as have been many high-ranking military officers. Since the 1980s, many Pashtuns have joined the police force, civil service and the military. Approximately 14 per cent of the top ranking officers of the army, the most powerful institution in the country, comprises people from the NWFP, mostly from Kohat and Mardan districts. In addition, they substantially control the country's transport network.

To check any possible separatist tendencies among the Pashtuns, successive federal governments have followed a policy of appeasement towards the province, and were the most favoured by the military. As a result, it has been among the fastest growing economies in Pakistan, unlike Sindh and Balochistan.

The geo-political location of the province has determined its response towards vital issues, especially the situation in Afghanistan. The Pashtuns in the province share very strong affiliations with their counterparts in Afghanistan. This factor was witnessed even during the elections in 2002, when Pashtun nationalist parties faced a major setback for the first time. Present day Pashtun nationalist leaders like Khan Abdul Wali Khan of Awami National Party, Ajmal Khattak of National Awami Party Pakistan, Afzal Khan and Mahmood Khan Achakzai of Pakhtunkhwa Milli Awami Party could not foresee this change in the political approach of Pashtuns in favour of a religious coalition, the Muttahida Majlis-e-Amal (MMA).

For the first time since 1946 the province today has a single party government. MMA has thus gained political prominence for the first time. The party finished with 11.3 per cent of the total polled votes at the national level, while it swept NWFP with 45.5 per cent of votes and 29 seats. It almost wiped out the ANP and the PPP who have alternatively won the NWFP elections in the past.

The political implications of the rise of MMA in NWFP are two-fold:

- MMA's attempt to fashion their own Islamic state in NWFP may have far reaching repercussions for national politics as well as the existing state structures. This is reflected in the Sharia Bill passed by the NWFP assembly;
- MMA's stance on foreign policy issues, especially pertaining to the US war on terrorism and Muslim causes may keep the federal government under pressure.

So far, the public expression of MMA policies in NWFP has amounted to little else besides pulling down cinema boards bearing pictures of women artists, attempting to chase musicians out of their traditional berths, banning male coaches for sportswomen. In fact, after over a year in power, there have been neither substantial changes nor benefits that the province has received. It has not been able to get rid of FBI presence in the country, nor has a single member been reported to cross into Afghanistan after the US bombings.

Unlike in the past, when the MMA's constituent parties worked to destabilise the political process, the coalition is now a stakeholder in the political process. Though MMA leaders have raised slogans against military operations in the tribal belt, the leaders at the federal level have objected to the Legal Framework Order of General Musharraf and his holding on to two posts, the formation of National Security Council, etc, but their willingness to negotiate on these contentious issues reflects their readiness to compromise.

Beyond doubt, the MMA will forge a partnership with the establishment as they had always done in the past for power sharing.

Clearly, the challenges facing NWFP society are tribalism versus modernism or forces of change. However, it is the liberal educated Pathans who would prevail.

Prospects

Growth

NWFP's economy is a classic case of growth without development. It has a reasonably good rate of growth in per capita income, has intensive involvement of donor agencies and receives enough funds from expatriates and Arab nations. However, the province lacks in critical development and significant income-generating activities.

The agriculture sector in NWFP is a major employer in the state, but not a significant revenue earner. Tobacco is the only major cash crop for the province. Agriculture has never been NWFP's forte. Though its largest area is under wheat cultivation, it has to import wheat from other provinces to meet its requirements. The government is also not looking at the province as a major agriculture hub.

Neither is the industrial sector developed. The economy mainly functions on the services sector. This sector is however highly sensitive to international developments and any adverse situation can have a magnified impact on the economy. This was clearly visible during the Afghan war in 2001, which eroded the services industry, including trade, transport and tourism.

Hydropower and minerals sector are being viewed as major drivers in boosting economic growth. With numerous rivers flowing in the province, hydropower can become a major source of environmentally clean energy. However, this entails building dams, which is proving difficult to undertake at the moment. Also, several projects in the water sector are facing major financial crunch and will need foreign investments. Similar is the case with the mineral sector of NWFP.

For being able to attract investments, NWFP has to project itself as an attractive destination. Islamisation of the province is bound to impact the economy on several fronts. Any form of radicalisation will deter investments in major employment-generating economic activities. However, the western countries will continue to pump in more funds in the socio-political sectors with the hope to change people's mindset so as to stem complete radicalisation of society, like the Taliban in Afghanistan.

The social sector would flourish, as Islamic society's provide an effective social safety net for its people. However, unemployment and poverty may be difficult to curb, as employment-generating economic activities would be limited.

Economic disempowerment of women will confine them to household activities, thus leading to under-utilisation of human resources. In an Islamic society, there can be no free flow of information thus leading to economic degradation. Worse, religious indoctrination will produce radical aggressive youth creating frequent law and order problems, and an increase in sectarian violence.

God

The real danger of MMA's win in NWFP is that it would unleash a wave of vigilante Islam: religious zealots trying to enforce whatever narrow notions and interpretations they have of an Islamic system and way of life. The Islamisation process of MMA is myopic, with scant regard for long-term repercussions.

The Islamisation of NWFP society will hit women the hardest. For mullahs, all evil begins with women. There are already talks about banning co-education schools, colleges and universities. Blasphemy laws will be more vigorously applied, the minorities will come under greater threat.

Activists linked to the alliance have forced girls school in the *chilas* area to shut down and have expelled NGOs. Reports from women working for NGOs in NWFP of harassment are widespread. Groups working for the uplift of communities, including the Sarhad Rural Support Programme, have faced increasing harassment due to their women-oriented schemes.

If MMA neglects women concerns and issues, the long-term effect of MMA government on women in the two provinces will be manifold:

- Tribalism in the name of Islam will aggravate violence, abuse and discrimination against women.

- The economic contribution of female will be curtailed..
- Co-education will be discouraged leading to lesser educational opportunities.
- The tradition-ridden, highly conservative society of NWFP will further impinge upon the rights of women as it will be backed and supported by the government forces.
- There is no women minister in the cabinet of the two provinces. Mere presence of 17 per cent women in the provincial assembly with no say in the policy making will not bring a change in the lives of women of NWFP and Balochistan.
- The government control electronic media in NWFP particularly will be used to disseminate a passive, docile, housewife role of women taking care of children only.
- There are widespread anti-Islamic practices like honor-killings about which the MMA has chosen to keep quiet.. The plight of women in NWFP and Balochistan will be more pathetic if MMA continues to ignore such anti-women practices.
- The policy of segregation has been put into effect. A plan for separate women university, medical college and sports directorate is in the pipeline.

However, it will be difficult for MMA to reconcile their contradictory stance on gender issues. Some of the parties within MMA support the idea of women's work, while there are some who want abolishing of co-education. The MMA is reluctant to take a clear stand on establishing segregation in the society due to fear of rejection.

Governance

The exceptional win of MMA in the October 2002 elections in NWFP marks the beginning of a tussle between modernity and religious orthodoxy in Pakistan. Socio-economic hardships and political uncertainty supplemented by the military government's decision to allow US troops to operate from Pakistani territory ensured the success of this religious group. In a way, the support of certain powerful institutions in the country also paved way for their success.

For the first time, a coalition of fiercely religious and *jihadi* groups have managed to win a mandate. The MMA cannot let go this opportunity to entrench and establish the rule of the clerics and gradually spread the influence to other parts of the country. The MMA so far has only partly succeeded in its endeavour.

On gaining power, the foremost step taken was to fashion their Islamic state. The party succeeded in passing the Shariah Bill. It introduced the Hasba (Accountability) Act, which is also in the pipeline. Beyond this, there has been no major initiative towards development. The party has failed on the economic front in being able to generate employment. At present, the party has changed its rhetoric of economic growth, and rather imputed economic underdevelopment to federal government antipathy.

On the political front, the MMA has eroded its credibility by compromising with the federal ruling party pertaining to the Legal Framework Order. This erosion is clearly visible in the rallies and protest meetings called by the MMA, where the attendance has drastically shrunk. Equivocal statements and belying actions have cast a shadow on MMA's credibility, and its governing capabilities.

The MMA has always taken pride in its ability to mobilise street power to galvanize federal government policies. The huge madrassa network has faithfully served MMA's public-hoodwinking gestures.

Apart from people's support receding, MMA's policies even counter federal goverment's own commitments. This will keep the two in perpetual confrontation. However, the relationship shared between the MMA-military-ML (Q) is still difficult to comprehend. Evidently, the MMA is still close to the establishment for every political decision of the military is conveyed to the MMA.

Nevertheless, the success of MMA hints at the tightening of the *jihadi* trap around Pakistan. The *jihadi* groups within

Pakistan have now found a legitimate platform to promote their ideology. However, the Pakistan government is under tremendous international pressures to curb the influence of the MMA and revamp the madaris network.

Some policies proposed by the MMA are a cause of serious concern particularly in urban areas. For example, the banning of co-education in schools and colleges could lead to a serious vacuum in female professionals in the long term - particularly in fields like health and education. The potential banning of satellite and cable TV in certain provinces might lead professionals and business to abandon urban areas like Peshawar in favour of other provinces.

Clerics have entered politics with a heavy baggage of orthodox ideas. From weekly holiday to the modes of public entertainment, and from economy to country's foreign engagements or disengagements, they want to get everything reshaped and reoriented as per requirement of their version of Islamic ideology. If they soften the rhetoric – 'Islam in danger', they are likely to lose their support base. Otherwise, they are likely to lose much of political relevance. To be or not to be, this is the real paradox. A number of factors put them and the country in an odd equation that might be described as zero sum game. This is a dangerous situation, potentially leading to polarisation.

Geopolitics

A major foreign factor affecting NWFP would be the situation in Afghanistan. In fact it is an inter-dependent phenomenon. This is primarily due to the Pashtun communality running across the borders.

The changes within NWFP, on MMA's coming to power, made the interim government in Afghanistan highly cautious. In reaction to MMA's win, the Afghan government set up new army camps to monitor border areas. It also set up additional check-posts and has been trying to gain support of tribal leaders along the borders, including those in Pakistan.

This fear is well founded on the side of Afghanistan, for constituents within the MMA are known to be highly influential in the Pashtun belt in Afghanistan, and support the Taliban. Maulana Fazlur Rehman, leader of JUI (F), is considered as the *de facto* spiritual father of the Pashtuns. Hence, if MMA is antagonised, they may whip-up the Pashtun sentiments in the border areas in Pakistan and Afghanistan and try to create a separate Pashtun state.

Further, Afghanistan's internal situation itself is quite shaky. In case Afghanistan breaks-up on ethnic basis, then the Pashtuns may rise against the Afghan government in favour of merging with Pakistan, or the entire Pashtun belt might demand independent statehood.

Another factor that can irk the Pashtuns and give rise to secessionist tendencies is the presence of American forces in the region. If Pakistan allows US troops to continue operationing in the region and also interfere in the Pashtun's affairs, this can lead to a major upheaval, and an armed struggle against the Pak government cannot be ruled out.

With the MMA coming to power, the western countries are watching Pakistan's military activities all the more intently. The recent debacle with regard to nuclear proliferation, and the targeting of Pakistan's nuclear scientists, has marked Pakistan's nuclear facilities unsafe. The Western media has not missed an opportunity to express fears that these facilities would fall into the hands of religious fundamentalists. As for nuclear weapons, these are controlled by the military, which will not entertain political intervention. Even if the US decides to control Pakistan's nuclear facilities, MMA can do nothing except stage public rallies in protest. Washington would anyway be negotiating with the Pakistan military, rather unmindful of MMA.

In NWFP, thus, secessionist tendencies can emerge only due to international factors, especially the situation in Afghanistan.

Forecast

NWFP will be a territorial base for the ideological conflict between economic modernisation and social orthodoxy; and specifically for the ambition of orthodox forces to rule Pakistan.

Trend

1) Gradual Islamisation of NWFP, resulting in an erosion in the status of women
2) Resistance to foreign investments, slowdown in industrialisation, boost in illegal trade.
3) Growth of *jihadi* forces will lead to a distortion in the education system with emphasis laid on setting up madaris. Also, there will be an increase in youth lacking skills of modern economy thus raising vested interests in developing religious institutions.
4) Close relations between MMA leaders and the Saudi leadership will restrain the scope of Pakistan leaders to take action against MMA, thereby enabling groups within MMA to increase their influence.

Discontinuity

1) If the middle-east situation deteriorates to such an extent that it is unable to absorb emploment, and repatriates those already living there, it will have an adverse impact on NWFP economy.
2) If Afghanistan disintegrates, the Pakhtoonistan movement will gain momentum and strain Pakistan's unity.
3) Operations in FATA along with increasing US interference will backlash on the army

Wild Card

1) In case of a conflict between Afghanistan and Pakistan, the geopolitical status of NWFP will change.
2) In case, US takes over Pakistan's federal government to forestall a national collapse, NWFP will seek separation.

CHAPTER 6

Sindh

Sindh is the third largest province in Pakistan covering 140,914 sq km, accounting for 17.7 per cent of the country's total area. With Karachi, as its capital, the province comprises of five administrative divisions and seventeen districts, which house nearly 23 per cent of the country's population.

Sindh derives its name from its only river Indus, locally known as *Sindhu.* Located in the southern-most tip of the country, the Indus forms its delta in the province before joining the Arabian Sea. The province is connected with areas of marked geographical contrasts. On the west lies the arid Balochistan in the north lies Punjab, to the east are the deserts of Indian Rajasthan and to the south are the Arabian Sea and the Rann of Kutch.

The people of Sindh greatly revere the Indus River, which they believe has created and sustains the province. These sentiments are well placed. Sindh falls in the arid/semi-arid zone, and has historically been receiving low rainfall, and the river has played a crucial role in nourishing life. The Indus delta has several lakes, which are rich in aquatic life. The Indus River in Sindh is home to the only surviving blind Dolphins in the world. The coastline has one of the biggest arid zone mangrove forests in the world. Apart from the ecological benefits, the river sustains Sindh's agrarian economy.

Sindh holds a very unique position – historically, politically and economically. It has acquired the distinction of being called *Bab-ul-Islam* (Gateway to Islam), as it was the first province to accept Islam in the subcontinent. Sindh also acts as a gateway for Pakistan to the international trade community as the only two major ports – Karachi and Port Qasim – in the country are located in the province.

The Sindhis are non-violent, but fiercely conscious of their ethnic identity. They have historically enjoyed cultural freedom and been able to develop a Sindhi consciousness. In spite of several invasions, they have managed to retain their culture and heritage, resisting the influence of any ethnic group. The province has a very rich heritage and culture that dates back seven millennia starting with the Indus Valley Civilization. Islamic rule was introduced in the early 8th century AD when Mohammad Bin Qasim conquered Sindh from its Hindu rulers.

During the British rule, Sindh was attached to Bombay Presidency till 1937, and following a movement for separation, it was made an autonomous province. It is believed that this separation of Sindh impelled the Muslim League to demand a separate Pakistan. Though Sindhis had chosen to join the Muslim League during the phase of the struggle, post 1946, the Sindhis were disillusioned with the Muslim League, and especially the leadership of Sir Mohammad Ali Jinnah, which led to the resignation of two very prominent Sindhi leaders from the League – Sheikh Abdul Majid and G M Syed.

G M Syed while presenting Sindh's case during his deposition in court stated: "A critical phase began in the political life of Sindh when the Cabinet Mission announced its plan in May 1946.....According to its proposals, the centre was to manage foreign affairs, communications and defence on behalf of the provinces, and all other matters were to be in the hands of the sub-federation. In our sub-federation, the Punjab because of being the majority province, would dominate. In the constituent assembly, Sindh was to get four seats in a house of thirty-eight. The result was inevitable: The Punjabis would make a Constitution of their own choice on the strength of their majority and Sindh would be subjugated by them. This would have curtailed the Sindhis independence, autonomy and disregard their aspirations.....This was a plan for the cremation of Sindh."

Sindh Muslims had chosen to join with Pakistan on the basis of the Lahore Resolution of 1940 brought out by the All India Muslim League in its twenty-seventh annual session on March 23, 1940, and commonly known as the 'Pakistan Resolution'. The declaration stated: "...areas in which the Muslims are numerically in a majority as in the Northwestern and Eastern zones of India should be grouped to constitute 'Independent States' in which the constituent units shall be autonomous and sovereign." The entire spirit of this resolution was lost once independence was attained for the 'independent states' were not allowed to remain autonomous and sovereign.

By then, partition came. Sindhi Muslims were unsure of their decision to join with Pakistan. Many of the educated elite and middle class of Sindh being Hindus and Sikhs had migrated to India, while a large number of Urdu-speaking Muslim migrants had arrived from India, known as *mohajirs*. This drastically transformed the ethnic composition in the province.

Due to the change in the ethnic composition, Sindhis were also seen losing their independence in some areas. The decision of the government in 1954 to merge all the provinces into "one unit" further eroded Sindh's sovereignty. At the time of the merger, Sindh had a surplus in its budget while Punjab was running a deficit. The merger deprived Sindh of its fiscal space, and was forced to share its revenues with the other provinces.

Later, even when the Unitary System was dissolved, the federal government continued to take away a large part of Sindh's revenues. Moreover, the appointment of several Punjabis to prominent posts, and Sindh's own lack of representation in the army and other important institutions, led to discriminatory feelings rising further.

This greatly irked the Sindhi population, which has felt deeply betrayed by the Urdu-speaking majority. This was the genesis for the *Jiye* Sindh movement, which shaped the Movement for Restoration of Democracy into a mass struggle in August-September 1983. The government directly confronted the Sindh revolt against military rule of General Zia-ul-Haq, and their demand for elections and restoration of the 1973 Constitution, with the army being called in to brutally suppress the movement. Nearly 500 civilians were killed amidst massive destruction of physical assets.

Following this incident, the federal government was seen consciously undermining Sindh. This reached a peak during General Zia-ul-Haq's regime. All Sindh governments since 1977 have proved to be incompetent and the ethnic massacres and riots during the days of Zia-ul-Haq have left deep scars on Sindh. This long spell of instability and violence has led to economic stagnation.

The dissent is still visible in Sindh, though in a smaller magnitude. The agitations by various regional parties still rake up the issue of the 1940 agreement, and its present status in Pakistan. There are clear signs of dissent in their rhetoric. However, these demands largely reflect Sindh's present socio-economic conditions.

In recent years, the money-spinner, Karachi, has been in the throes of major sectarian, ethnic and terrorist incidents. The economic situation is also deteriorating, with visible widespread signs of de-industrialisation, apart from water shortages affecting agriculture. Further, the provincial government is under tremendous fiscal constraints, though its revenue generation far exceeds its expenditure. Most Sindhis believe that they have not received an equitable share in Pakistan's national resources, while their own resources have been usurped for the benefit of other provinces.

Table 6.1: Sindh's Ethnic Composition

(% share)

Area	Urdu	Punjabi	Sindhi	Pushto	Balochi	Seraiki	Others
Rural	0.8	1.4	47.2	0.3	0.8	0.0	0.6
Urban	20.3	6.0	12.5	3.9	1.3	1.0	4.3
Total	20.8	7.4	59.7	4.2	2.1	1.0	4.9

Sindh is Pakistan's fault line. The Sindhis have a number of grievances against the federal government and Punjab. Their grouses range from not receiving due share of water and financial resources, to anti-Sindh projects of the federal government, to environmental degradation in the Indus basin, to increased law and order problems. There has been excessive politicisation, leading to severe financial and economic constraints, despite having a strong agricultural base effectively complemented by the industrial and commercial capital Karachi.

Population

Sindh's population grew from 14 million in 1972 to 35 million in 1973, and is likely to touch 42 million by 2010. The population growth rate has declined from an average of 3 per cent during the inter-census period of 1972-81 to 2.8 per cent during the period 1981-98. Sindh, the second most populated province after Punjab and houses 23 per cent of the countrys total population. Karachi is the most populous division of the provinces accounting for 32 per cent of the provincial population.

Within Karachi, central Karachi is the most thickly populated with a density of 33,014 people per sq km, followed by east Karachi with a density of 19,755 persons per sq km and south Karachi with a density of 14,303 persons per sq km. This division also has the highest population growth rate of 3.6 per cent, much higher than the provincial average.

Nearly 53 per cent of Sindh's population is below the age-group of 19 years and their literacy levels exceed 54 per cent. Of these, nearly 8 million or 28 per cent of the total population will join the workforce by 2010. Given Sindh's economic stagnation, absorption of this imminent burgeoning workforce would be a daunting task.

Sindh has the highest level of urbanisation in the country at 49 per cent, thanks to concentrated development around Karachi that houses 66 per cent of Sindh's urban population. It is interesting to note that if one excludes Karachi, the level of urbanisation in Sindh declines to 28 per cent. The other urban centres in Sindh include Sukkur and Hyderabad districts. The disparity between rural and urban centres in Sindh is very sharp. Excluding Karachi, poverty and underdevelopment in rural Sindh is highest compared to the other provinces.

The Sindhi ethnic group constitutes a dominating 60 per cent of the total provincial population. The Urdu-speaking Mohajirs who comprise about 21 per cent of the population, come next in order. Only 13 per cent of Sindhis live in the urban areas, while the rest are in the rural areas. The Mohajir population is largely concentrated in the urban areas, especially Karachi.

The influx of Muslim migrants from India, known as mohajirs (refugees in Urdu) changed the demographic balance of the province. From 1947 to 1955, the cities of Karachi, Hyderabad, Sukkur and Mirpurkhas became strongholds of Urdu-speaking migrants. The Sindhis resented the growing influence of Urdu language and culture. The general elections in December 1970 clearly highlighted the ethnic division with the rural areas voting for the Sindhi-dominated party, PPP, and the urban areas voting for Urdu-speaking candidates. The dominance gained by the mohajirs in the urban areas and their non-assimilation of the Sindhi culture widened the rift between the two ethnic groups, increasing social tensions. The language riots in 1972 was an attempt by the Sindhis in self-assertion.

While the Sindhi culture remained aligned to rural feudal traditions, mohajirs had a more urban-middle class background. As a result, the two distinct cultures cannot coexist. The Mohajirs primarily belonged to the business, trade and other professional fields, and their educational edge, vis-à-vis the native Sindhi population, paved way for their prominent role in the administration of the province. However, the equations changed when Zulfikar Ali Bhutto during his rule framed a policy marking 60 per cent of state jobs to rural areas and 40 per cent to urban areas. The Sindhi Prime Minister's policy of promoting the interests of the native Sindhis led to the formation of the Mohajir Quami Movement (MQM).

Between 1972 and 1977 there were several violent conflicts between the two ethnic groups. With the dismissal of the Bhutto government, the Sindh-Mohajir conflict took a new turn. General Zia-ul-Haq did not make any attempt to resolve the Sindh-Mohajhir conflict. With the influx of Pathans and Punjabis to Sindh during the 1980s, the mohajirs authority in the urban areas was eroded. Pathans took over the road transport business whereas Punjabis entrenched themselves in the employment circuit. This created a sense of insecurity amongst the mohajirs. In August 1986, Altaf Hussain, the leader of mohajirs, in a huge public meeting in Karachi, accused Punjab of marginalising Mohajirs and Sindhis and called for unity between the two ethnic groups. Unprecedented indications of reconciliation between the two groups surfaced – albeit for a brief period. Between 1988-1990, Sindh saw the bloodiest ethnic violence in its history between the Mohajirs and Sindhis, which consumed several lives.

In recent years, however, there has been a marked shift in the relations between the mohajirs and the Sindhis. The two factions are relatively more tolerant and coexisting. They are united on several important provincial issues like water distribution and allocation of financial resources by the centre. The MQM has managed to carve out a role for itself in national politics with representation in the federal government. For the first time in many years, organised effort is supplanting historic mistrusts.

Economy

Sindh has an edge over other provinces on several counts, principally higher literacy rates and richness of human and natural resources. The province plays a leading role in the oil and gas sector. Sindh is home to the Karachi port – Pakistan's gateway to the world – that makes the province the largest contributor to the national exchequer.

In spite of such high revenue earning capabilities of the province, it suffers from liabilities and a debt burden of Rs.106 billion. This is primarily due to the exceptional transfer of funds from Sindh through a variety of modes. This can be blamed on the federal fiscal structure whereby revenue collections in Sindh are higher than allocations for development as well as fixed expenditure.

Sindh can be divided into four economic zones: the industrialised and developed Karachi, the irrigated belt along the Indus River, the arid belt along its right bank, and the desert belt in the east and southeast. The heterogeneity in Sindh's economy has led to vast disparities between the urban and rural centres. Karachi presents one picture; and the rest of the province is a flagrant contrast.

Agriculture is Sindh's core activity producing cash crops like

Table 6.2: Sindh's Role in Pakistan's Economy

	% share
Value of international trade	90
Customs duties collection	80
Income tax collection	65
Central excise duty collections	35
Federal exchequer	63
Large scale industries	34
Manufacturing sector	68
Agriculture to Agro-GDP	23
Crude oil production	62
Natural gas production	48

cotton, sugarcane, wheat, rice and fish. This primary activity contributes about 25-30 per cent to the total provincial GDP. However, this sector has been severely affected by drought conditions prevailing since 1996, which has led to agricultural losses to the tune of Rs.42 billion. Industrial activity does exist in Sindh, albeit with a high concentration in Karachi, and partly in Hyderabad. About 75 per cent of the software houses in Pakistan are in Karachi.

Karachi holds a very unique position in Sindh. Though technically a part of Sindh, it has an identity radically different from the rest of the province. It is the commercial and industrial hub of Pakistan. Economic indicators of Sindh do depict a picture of prosperity. However, the edifice of Sindh's economy stands entirely upon Karachi. The economic vibrancy that Sindh appears to be savouring is indeed that of Karachi. In a general sense, worldwide, epicentres of growth do exist. However, over time, there is always a spillover effect by which development cascades into neighbouring areas, setting into motion a phenomenon of overall economic upliftment. In the case of Sindh, sadly, this is not the case. The rapid strides of Karachi's development have not landed outside the commercial hub. The rest of Sindh has remained fairly insular to Karachi's progress, to the extent that it is actually retrograding in the face of Karachi's forward march.

At the time of independence, certain intrinsic advantages made Karachi the focal point of the incipient industrialisation in Pakistan. The growth was rapid, and by 1965, around 44 per cent of large scale manufacturing was concentrated here. In the late 1960s, the government followed a deliberate policy of discouraging further industrialisation in Karachi. This led to growth centres beginning to emerge in other parts of the country, especially Punjab.

Since 1985, Karachi has been at the hub of political, ethnic, and sectarian violence, which has restrained economic development.

During the 1990s, though the entire country was affected by poor growth performance, Sindh suffered the most. Its growth in per capita income at 1.8 per cent per annum was much lower than the actual population growth rate, thus implying a massive increase in poverty levels. Investment has been slow to come to Karachi and also other parts of Sindh due to law and order problems. This has benefited the Punjab and Dubai, where industry and investment have shifted.

The de-industrialisation process in Sindh had picked up in 2001, affecting job opportunities in urban areas. An official survey revealed that employment in the industrial sector had dropped by 2.5 per cent during July 2001 to March 2002. Growth in industrial production was an insignificant 0.3 per cent. Persisting drought, crippling tax structure imposed under the influence of World Bank-IMF, fluctuations in exchange value of rupee, breakdown of infrastructure and growing lawlessness were blamed for the closure of several industries in the province.

The increased migration into Karachi resulted in the proliferation of slums (known as *katchi abadis),* shantytowns, and traffic congestion. Severe water shortages exacerbated the adversity. The multi-ethnic blend of Karachi is also proving to be an impediment, giving rise to ethnic and sectarian violence due to growing unemployment and worsening socio-economic conditions.

Agriculture

Sindh is the second largest contributor to the agriculture sector of Pakistan, after Punjab. Its contribution is a significant 23 per cent to total agricultural GDP of the country. Primarily an agrarian economy, 43 per cent of the population depend on this sector for its livelihood.

Approximately 40 per cent of Sindh's geographical land or 5.6 million hectares is under cultivation, of which nearly 60 per cent is irrigated. Since Sindh falls in the arid/semi-arid zone, canal irrigation plays a crucial role. Canal water supplies are in turn dependent on the flows in the river Indus. Moreover, around 75 per cent of Sindh's groundwater resources are brackish and unfit for irrigation. It has only about 2.6 million acres of fresh groundwater to supplement its erratic surface water supplies.

Cotton, rice, sugarcane and wheat are the main crops produced in Sindh. Since rice is the only crop that can be grown in the inundated lands within the delta of the Indus, it is by far the most important crop cultivated in the province. Sindh's contribution to rice production in the country is a significant 41 per cent

Fishing is another important activity with 70 per cent of Pakistan's marine production coming from Sindh. Fruit production in the province accounts for 13.2 per cent of the country's total. Mangoes grown in the province have high export value.

Larkana district is the highest producer of fine quality rice followed by Jacobabad, Sukkur, Badin, Thatta and Dadu districts. Cotton is produced mainly in central parts of Sindh in Sanghar, Nawabshah, and Hyderabad. Sugarcane is another important crop, mainly grown in the Kotri Barrage zone in the south.

Agriculture being crucial to the economy of Sindh, its security is of utmost importance. However, Sindh has been exposed to the vagaries of nature, with intermittent drought and floods. The floods of July 2003 played havoc damaging approximately 229,754 acres of crop area. Apart from natural mishaps, Sindh also suffers from man-made complexities like salinity and waterlogging, affecting about 88 per cent of its agricultural land. The weak irrigation network in Sindh has led to waterlogged agricultural lands, which has affected crop production further. The worst phase has been the drought period of 1996-2002

Economic Journey of Provinces

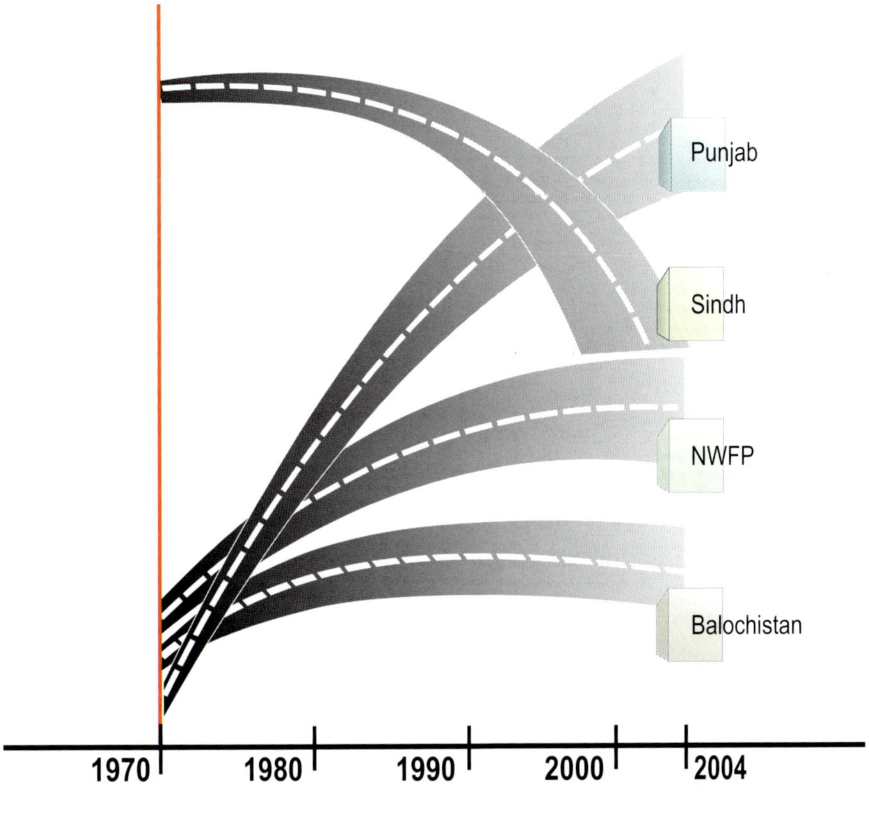

Water Resources in Sindh

Sindh has three water barrages located on the Indus River – Sukkur, Guddu and Kotri – which are over four decades old and lack maintenance. Sindh depends on canal irrigation to the extent of 95 per cent of its requirements, as groundwater resources have become unfit for irrigation. About 5.6 million hectares is cultivable in the province, of which about 2.6 to 3 million hectares is commanded by canals, 0.15 million hectares by tube-wells and 0.5 million hectares by other sources of irrigation.

Sindh has an inherent geographical disadvantage of being located at the extreme end of the Indus Basin. It has historically received low rainfall – an average 165 mm per year – that has resulted in an oddity. When it needs water, it does not get sufficient supply and when it does not need water (during floods), all the excess water of the upper river stream is flushed into Sindh.

Sindh has only one source of water – the Indus River. The average annual withdrawal from the three existing barrages for irrigation is around 45 MAF, combined for rabi and kharif crops. Water is conveyed through a network of canals, branch canals, distributaries and minors and ultimately passes through more than 4,200 watercourses.

Reduced water flows in the Indus and the ongoing drought have meant severe irrigation water-cuts. Sindh's share in irrigation water was cut by 25 per cent, 43 per cent, 28 per cent and 54 per cent in four consecutive seasons in the two years from 2000 to 2002. In 2002-2003, due to above normal rainfall, water shortages were lower at 18 per cent and 34 per cent during kharif and rabi seasons respectively. In areas like Khairpur, Dadu and lower Larkana, river flows have receded to such an extent that the riverbed is being cultivated.

The early signs of devastating effects of water scarcities are already visible in Sindh –sea intrusion, declining marine life and erosion of the delta region. Sea intrusion has already destroyed 1.2 million acres of farmland. Only 10 per cent of the Indus delta exists at present. Till 1978, the Indus delta area had timber forests spread over 2.63 lakh hectares. This area came down to 1.58 lakh hectares in 1990. At present, the timber forest area is just four lakh acres and is proving disastrous to marine life.

There are striking disparities in the agricultural losses suffered by Sindh and Punjab. While Punjab managed to increase its cropped area during the drought period, Sindh's area under cultivation has drastically declined. Sindh is estimated to have suffered agricultural losses to the tune of Rs.42 billion in only three years – 2001 to 2003.

Since May 2002, the province has been contending with another adversity – a deteriorating canal network. There have been over 70 incidents of deep and wide cracks developing in canals from June 2002 to early 2004. Only 6 per cent of the watercourses in Sindh are lined, as compared with 70 per cent in Punjab. Also, the Sukkur barrage has developed technical faults due to lack of maintenance.

Agitations against water shortages and water riots have become commonplace. Also, antagonism to contentious water projects – the Kalabagh dam and the Thal canal – has intensified.

Sindh, unlike Punjab, has never received due consideration in water-related matters. However, during General Musharraf's regime, for the first time, water development projects were envisaged for Sindh. In early 2003, General Musharraf promised a package of Rs.13 billion to Sindh to revamp its irrigation system. However, till end-2003, no funds were disbursed.

Meanwhile, Sindh has been receiving tremendous aid from the Asian Development Bank and World Bank for renovating its water facilities. World Bank has offered a loan of $1 billion for improving the water system in the province. The Sindh government has drawn up plans to construct 10 small dams, line watercourses and increase the capacity of Sukkur barrage. Projects worth $28 billion were approved for lining of canals in the province, which can increase water flows by about 40 per cent.

In 2001, faced with multiplicity of interests and serious concerns of opposition emanating from Sindh, the military government of General Musharraf tried to correct these discrepancies. One of the primary reasons for the government to take these decisions in Sindh's favour was to gain consensus with regard to construction of large dams, especially Kalabagh, which is being vehemently opposed by the province.

On September 13, 2003, General Musharraf, in his first ever non-political address to the nation, appealed for supporting the construction of direly needed water storage projects for Pakistan's sustained economic progress. This speech was rendered at a time when Pakistan was facing severe opposition, primarily from Sindh, to the undertaking of large dams. The underlying desperation to take up large water storage projects was prominent in General Musharraf's address to the nation. Resistance from provinces has been the root cause of Pakistan's inability to undertake large water storage projects.

Ever, since General Musharraf announced the building of Kalabagh dam, there has been turmoil in Sindh. Rallies and demonstrations are being held with disturbing regularity. Many politicians have questioned the military's right to rule. The provincial assembly also witnessed pandemonium and some politicians went to the extent of reminding the federal leadership of the break-up of the country in 1971.

Amidst political and inter-provincial uproar, General Musharraf has felt it imperative to address the nation on the water issue and discuss the importance of building large dams and overlook differences for a national cause. He said: "The verbal altercation between WAPDA and Sindh would never end but we would neglect their dispute and would concentrate on construction of dams." He appealed to the leadership of NWFP and Sindh to stop resisting construction of dams, as this was the only way Pakistan could make progress.

Referring to the grievances of Sindh, General Musharraf said: "We cannot live in the past. I apologise for the wrong doing to any province by any one in the past and assure that all provinces will get just and fair treatment in future" – spelling out clearly that provinces have been victims of unjust treatment at the hands of the Punjabi-dominated federal government.

Sindh has been frustrating Pakistan's endeavour of creating water storage facilities. Due to past experiences, Sindh is perennially wary of any storage or canal projects undertaken upstream as most projects have first favoured Punjab and then the other provinces.

The reactions emanating from across Sindh against projects envisaged for water development are a reflection of its edgy and defensive reaction towards Punjab and the Punjabi-dominated federal government. The Sindhi newspapers, Ibrat and Kawish, are reverberating with views of national disintegration if projects like Kalabagh dam are undertaken. Also, the elected representatives in the Sindh assembly are united against the project. Moreover, regional parties from NWFP and Balochistan are also joining with the Sindhi nationalist parties in their cause against the federal government.

For agriculture to progress, it is essential to undertake a major revamping of the irrigation network of Sindh, apart from setting up storage projects. However, the revitalizing of water resources will have to be in conjunction with Punjab's water sector development, for finally Sindh is heavily dependent on Punjab to release waters downstream.

Industry

Karachi is at the hub of industrial development in Pakistan. Sindh dominates the manufacturing scene, though the pace of development in the province has slowed down since the last two decades. Pakistan began with very little industry, but by the early 1960s, over 50 per cent of units were located in Sindh around Karachi.

However, in the mid-1960s, the government followed a conscious policy to discourage further industrialisation in Karachi.

This policy allowed the spread of industries to other regions in the country, especially Punjab. Today, Punjab has surpassed Sindh in the small-scale industrial sector.

The *Census of Manufacturing Industries* (CMI), which is conducted annually by the Federal Bureau of Statistics and provincial departments, lists the number of reporting industries for Karachi in 1995-96 (the latest year) as 1,062. Although, this is a clear huge under-reporting of economic activity in the city, it helps to see Karachi in the context of the province of Sindh. Karachi has 70 per cent of all listed industrial units as per CMI in Sindh, with an average daily employment of 142,813. While these actual figures are under-reported, what are worth looking at are some trends. While Karachi had 1,062 industrial units listed in 1995-96, this was less than the 1,219 listed in 1991-92, showing industrial decline and a closure of firms in this five-year period. Moreover, the Index of Industrial Production in Sindh has actually fallen: from 177.09 in 1991-92, to 170.37 in 1999-2000. In this ten-year period, it has been below this 1991-92 figure in all but one year. All indications of a stagnation in industrial production are borne out by this statistic.

Though Karachi's industrialisation has slowed down in recent years, it still continues to be the commercial capital and the most important industrial centre in the country. At present, the city generates about 15 per cent of the national GDP

Table 6.3: Industrial Units in Sindh - 1995

Division	No. of Industrial Units
Karachi	1062
Hyderabad.	151
Sukkur	82
Larkana	208
Mirpurkhas	25
Sindh	1528

Source: Sindh Bureau of Statistics

and contributes about 25 per cent to the federal revenue. It also generates 42 per cent of value added in large-scale manufacturing. It has the largest and most dynamic industrial complex in the country, which include SITE and Korangi Industrial & Trade Estate. A quarter of Pakistan's value added in the construction sector originates from Karachi. In terms of a contribution to the energy sector (electricity and gas), the transport, communications and storage sector, and the wholesale and trade sector, Karachi's contribution in each of these areas is at least 25 per cent of the country's value addition. Being the financial capital of Pakistan, the value addition that takes place in Karachi in the banking and insurance sector is almost half of that of the entire country.

The reasons why Karachi dominates in terms of economic and social indicators are not difficult to understand. The fact that it has Pakistan's largest port, that it was the federal capital for the first two decades after independence at a time when large-scale manufacturing was growing exponentially, and that it received a huge number of educated and skilled migrants following independence, helped in the establishing an economic base which has continued to be built upon over the last thirty years. With growth and development becoming considerably less spatially concentrated following the agricultural Green Revolution and the Middle East led boom, although Karachi has lost some of its economic supremacy, its dominance is unrivalled.

After the Indus River, Karachi forms the lifeline of Sindh's economy. However, the city has been a victim of politicisation, which has eroded its influence. According to reports, the 1983 insurgency marked the beginning of the process of de-industrialisation in the province. This was done by promoting industrial houses in Punjab like the Ittefaq group owned by the Sharief family. As a result, a major shift of industries was noticed during the 1980s and 1990s to Punjab and NWFP. During the period of General Zia-ul-Haq's regime, political victimisation of Karachi was at its peak, which resulted in a shift of manufacturing units outside Karachi. The shifting of industries out of Karachi is also discussed in Chapter 2 on inter-provincial comparisons.

In 2001, the first visible signs of de-industrialisation in Karachi came to light with a decline in industrial employment to the extent of 2.5 per cent. Due to recession in the late 1990s, nearly 4000 industrial units in Pakistan were declared sick, many of which were from Karachi.

Despite the decline in industrial growth in Sindh, manufacturing continues to play a significant role in the province's economy, employing 13.4 per cent of the population. There are over 20 industrial estates in the province with one in every division. Proximity to the port and commercial markets, along with the accessibility of labour and raw materials, has also been economically beneficial.

In recent years Sindh has witnessed closure of several industries in the province. Apart from this, the frequent water cuts, liquidity crunch, non-availability of fresh finance and volatile law and order situation has hampered investments, worsening the situation further.

Sindh has a daunting task to revive its sagging agricultural and industrial sectors – both sectors being victims of man-created situations. Sindh has a natural advantage in both the sectors, but seems to have been consciously undermined in its potential. The industrial sector of Sindh has been suffering from policy neglect, political plotting, natural calamities and a grossly ineffective provincial government. If the current stagnation continues, and the economy degenerates, Karachi will lose much of its existing shine of being the commercial, financial and trade hub of Pakistan.

Minerals

Along with agriculture and industry, Sindh is also rich in minerals. The southwestern regions of Sindh, especially those close to the Indus Delta, are endowed with ample energy resources such as oil, gas and coal, besides metallic minerals.

Sindh's energy resources are the most significant. It has the largest reserve of oil in the country with about 60 oilfields and 44 gas fields. Nearly 66 per cent of crude oil production comes from Sindh.

In late 2003, huge reserves of high quality oil were discovered at Noabad near Nawabshah. It is estimated that the new discovery would produce about 3,000 barrels of oil and 40 million sq feet of gas per day. The high quality oil contains 44 per cent super oil and 22 per cent of diesel proportion. The output, worth $70,000 per day, would strengthen the provincial as well as the national economy.

Sindh has the largest reserves of gas as well. In fact it is the highest producer of gas in the country. The biggest reserve is located near Mithi, in the southeastern part of the province. Nearly half the gas produced in Pakistan is from Sindh. Major gas fields have been discovered recently in Bhit and Zamzama in the Dadu district of Sindh, which also has a high concentration of low and medium temperature geo-thermal springs.

Table 6.4: Mineral Production in Sindh: 2000

Mineral	in Tonnes
Marble	22,048
Laterite	20,000
Celestite	10,560
Fuller's Earth	187,926
Gravel	110,844
Limestone	27,000,000
Red Ochre	7,050
Silica Sand	260,164
Crude Oil	1,739,700
Natural Gas	479,370*

*in million cubic feet

The province also has the largest coal reserves – over 95 per cent of Pakistan's mineable coal reserves are located in Sindh. The major coalfields of Sindh are Lakhra coalfield in Dadu district, Meting-Jhimpir in Thatta district, Sonda close to the national highway linking Karachi and Hyderabad and Thar in the Tharparkar district. The Thar area of Sindh is estimated to have 2.8 billion tonnes of coal reserves. However, most of the coalfields in Sindh are not yet developed, providing tremendous potential for foreign investment.

Apart from fuel resources, Sindh also has deposits of metallic and non-metallic minerals like laterite, clay, bauxite, limestone, dolomite, silica sand, marble and granite.

Sindh has had substantial earnings in the form of royalty for its fuel resources. In 2001, Sindh earned Rs.147.4 million as royalty. However, the areas where the minerals are located are highly underdeveloped and lack basic infrastructure like water and electricity. Development of the mining sector is a fairly new phenomenon. In fact, the agriculture and industrial sectors attracted most of the resources, much to the neglect of the mining sector. However, now since the agriculture and industrial sectors are facing a setback, the government has begun promoting the mining sector, which can also help in generating employment.

Relations with the Centre

Sindh's relations with the federal government have been explosive since its formation. It has been neglected and been a victim of wrong policy decisions, which has undermined its potential. The province is the highest revenue earner but continues to remain in deficit. Sindh too feels that policies are biased in favour of Punjab. Whether it is the issue on the allocations of National Finance Commission or policies on water, the Centre has always sidelined Sindh, whilst fulfilling the needs of Punjab.

Table 6.5: Sindh's Royalty Receipts: 2003

(In billions)

Gas	5.59
Surcharge	10.70
Oil	2.67

One dimly perceives that there has been a deliberate attrition of Sindh's economic prowess. Foremost is the federal set up which has eaten into Sindh's resources. The distribution of funds under the National Finance Commission clearly shows the transfer of financial resources from Sindh to the other provinces. Keeping population as the basis for distribution of funds from the divisible pool clearly reflects the protection being provided to a single province, which is the centre of the most powerful institution in Pakistan – the military. It has been during General Zia-ul-Haq's rule, that Sindh suffered the most from wilful political neglect that emaciated Sindh's polity.

The top positions in the provincial government largely consist of Punjabis. The corps commanders of Sindh are mostly from Punjab. The entire political set up in the province is influenced by Punjab. Top positions in the bureaucracy are mostly held by Punjabis. Only in 2004 were there visible signs of Sindh being a priority for development funds.

In the present set up, Sindh finances about 15 to 20 per cent of its expenses. About 81 per cent of its revenue comes from external sources. The current revenue receipts in the provincial Budget for 2003-04 were Rs.90.9 billion of which the provincial contribution was Rs.14.1 billion. This implies that the province contributed 16 per cent and relied on the federal government for the rest of the finances. Meanwhile, revenue earned by the federal government from Sindh amounts to about 68 per cent.

Sindh contributes 65 per cent to income tax collection, 80 per cent of customs duties and 35 per cent of the central excise duty. It is pertinent to mention here that all the provinces receive more than their contribution, all of course at the cost of Sindh.

The royalty received by Sindh from the federal government on account of gas, coal and oil (including surcharge) was around Rs.19 billion in 2003.

Though Sindh has the potential to be self-reliant, it is deprivation, rather than economic prosperity, that lies in store for the province. Discrimination in financial allocation has greatly irked Sindhis, especially the regional groups. Successive Sindh governments have failed to remedy the situation, which has justified the regional groups agitation against discrimination and their portent of a war-like situation as in 1971.

Although Sindh is as competent as Punjab at all levels – in trade, manufacturing and development – it finds itself marginalized when it comes to distribution of resources.

Since 2003-2004 there has been a marked change in the federal government's management towards the smaller provinces, especially Sindh. General Musharraf has gone to the extent of apologising for past mistakes and seeking reprieve from Sindh. He has been frequently visiting the province, assuring people of due rights. On February 13, 2004, the President cum COAS assured Sindh cabinet that Sindh would receive its due share of water and financial resources. He informed: "Before 2000, Punjab had 20 per cent share in the Public Sector Development Programme (PSDP) and Sindh had less than 10 per cent. But now, Sindh share in the PSDP was more than that of Punjab." He also assured due representation in the armed forces. Earlier, he also announced a package for the revamping and development of Karachi.

Better late than never! Evidently, the General feared that discrimination might galvanize Sindhis into a formidable force.

This is quite clear from the way regional groups like the Jeay Sindh Quami Movement, Sindh National Front and others, were unitedly fighting against water projects. Another ostensible reason could be to keep the most powerful regional party, the Pakistan People's Party, out of Sindh politics, and extend the influence of a Punjab-dominated party and the mohajirs to rule the province.

Political Management

The Pakistan People's Party is the most powerful political group in Sindh since the days of Zulfikar Ali Bhutto. Rural Sindh has been its stronghold. The party has ruled the province and on three occasions at the federal level. The elections in 2002 once again got the party the highest number of votes in the province. However, the PPP leader, Benazir Bhutto, being on self-exile, was unable to form the government. Political uncertainty persisted till early 2003 and finally General Musharraf managed to install a government of his choice - an ML (Q)-Muttahida Quami Movement (MQM - Altaf Hussain) coalition.

This was a glaring example of army manipulations in the politics of the province. The present governor of Sindh, Dr. Ishrat-ul-Ibad of the MQM, had been on exile for several years and had serious criminal charges against him. Prior to his appointment as governor, he was absolved of all charges. The army, in order to keep the PPP out of Sindh politics, struck an informal deal with the MQM and doled out several favours including the governorship of Sindh. In the past, the army had engineered a split in the original Mohajir Quami Movement, which led to the formation of MQM headed by Altaf Hussain.

The governor of Sindh has the backing of the army, while the Chief Minister, Ali Mohammad Meher, has been left visibly powerless.

Lately, there have been perceptible signs of the government trying to break the hold of PPP in rural Sindh. One such move has been the proposal to split Larkhana district in interior Sindh into two. This district is the stronghold of PPP party chief, Benazir Bhutto.

Clearly, till there is army rule in Pakistan, PPP will not be in a position to gain power in the province. Moreover, PPP projects itself more as a national party rather than a regional group.

The second largest party in the province is MQM. Till early 2002, MQM was mainly a regional party in Sindh with some presence in Punjab. However, since the elections, they have managed to carve out a role at the federal level as well. This has brought them into the national mainstream - thanks to the army.

Among, the regional groups, the most vociferous is the Jeay Sindh Quami Mahaz (JSQM), which has been very strongly agitating for Sindhi rights and is

Provinces' Contribution to National Exchequer

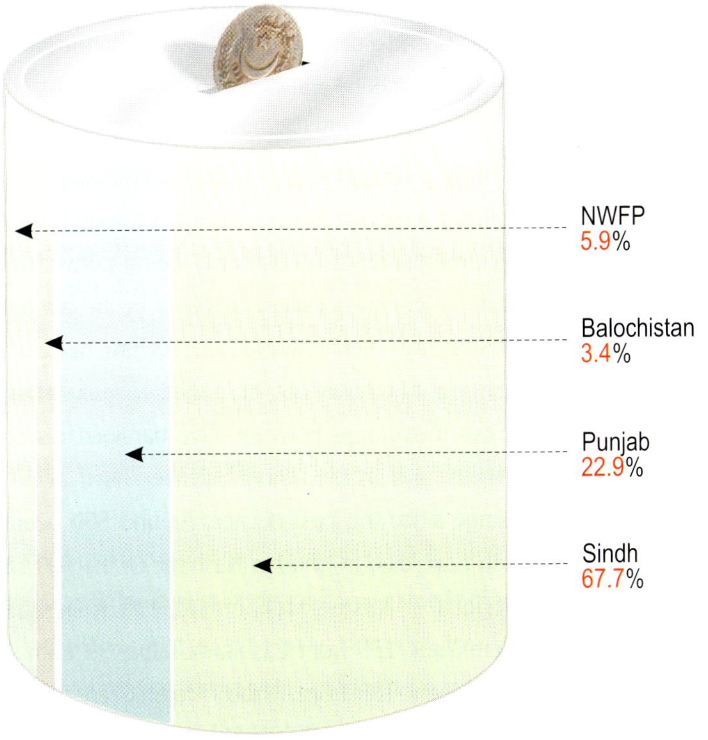

government insists on building Kalabagh dam and neglects Sindh's demands on the sharing of water and fiscal resources, the nationalist groups will receive an impetus. It will then depend on the quality of their leaders, and their ability to channelise mass protests. But who had guessed about Shaikh Mujibur Rehman five years before he arrived on the scene.

Geopolitics

Sindh is not of strategic importance to Pakistan. However, the port city of Karachi is and will continue to remain the important sea-route. The upcoming Gwadar port notwithstanding, Karachi's importance will subsist. Pakistan will therefore not easily cede the province.

If Sindh continues to suffer economic deterioration and water shortages, internal turmoil is inevitable. This can lead to a refugee inflow into India. However, such a situation cannot occur in the first half of the decade. Post 2007, which is when water scarcity would reach an unbearable proportion, such a situation cannot be ruled out unless Pakistan takes concrete measures to alleviate Sindh's misery.

The influx of Sindh refugees can bring India into direct confrontation with Pakistan. If there is influx into India, history threatens to repeat. Independent Sindh might be born but not before the 1971 war is replayed. If such a situation had to occur in Balochistan or NWFP, the refugee flow would have been to Iran and neighbouring states, obviating India's involvement.

Forecast

Shortage of water in the second-half of the decade will lead to low agricultural and industrial growth, high unemployment and high separatist tendencies.

Trend

1) Karachi port will continue to be a source of revenue for the federal government and the prime motivating factor for the federal leadership to prevent separation.
2) *Jihadis* will continue to grow in strength.

Discontinuity

1) Gradual economic transformation from its current forte in agriculture and industry to minerals and services.
2) Benazir Bhutto's return and MQM's deal with the army soured, ethnic strife between Sindhis and mohajirs will increase.
3) Shia-Sunni conflict will increase.
4) If the water situation worsens expeditiously, and fiscal allocations are not settled, separatist movements will gather strength.

Wild Card

Separation of Sindh leading to refugee inflow into India will force the neighbour's involvement in Pakistan.

CHAPTER 7

Punjab

Punjab - meaning the land of five rivers - is the richest, most fertile and most heavily populated province of Pakistan. It is known as the granary of Pakistan - contributing around 68 per cent to the country's foodgrain production, 70 per cent to vegetable production and 80 per cent to cotton production. It is primarily agrarian, though industry also makes a substantial contribution.

To the north of the Punjab lie North West Frontier Province (NWFP) and the federal capital Islamabad. To the northeast is the Kashmir under Pakistani jurisdiction, to the east and south is India (Indian Punjab and Rajasthan), and to the southwest lie Sindh, and to the west are Balochistan and NWFP.

All the major rivers of the country - Indus, Jhelum, Chenab, Ravi and Sutlej - flow through this province. The province is predominantly on level plain, although some mountainous hilly areas are found in the northwest and extreme southwest. There is a plateau adjacent to the mountains known as Potohar plateau and a desert belt, Cholistan, in the southeast.

Punjab extends over an area of 2,05,344 sq km which makes it the second largest province in Pakistan accounting for 25.8 per cent of total land area. The province comprises of eight administrative divisions and 34 districts. The predominant religion in the Punjab is Islam, with a small Christian minority. Punjabi is the mother tongue of 90 per cent of the population.

The major ethnic groups in the Punjab include Jat, Rajput, Arian, Gujar and Awaran. While Urdu is the official language of the province, there are several local dialects –Punjabi, Potohari, Seraiki, Jatki and Jangli.

By its sheer strength - in terms of population, geographical area and economy - Punjab exerts heavy influence on Pakistan's socio-economic performance.

Population

Population growth in the province during the inter-censal period of 1971 to 1981 was 2.32 per cent. However, in the period 1981 to 1998, the rate grew to 2.64 per cent. Punjab is the only province where population growth rate has actually increased. All other provinces have either shown a decline in population expansion or have witnessed stagnant levels during the two inter-censal periods.

This present average population growth rate implies a total population of 82.7 million in 2003, and over 100 million by 2011.

In 1998, population density in the province was 353 persons per sq km as compared to the national average of 164. Punjab's population density touched 402 persons per sq km in 2003, and is expected to reach 496 persons per sq km in 2011.

Punjab thus faces a tremendous task of having to keep pace with its rapidly rising population which not only adds pressures on the resources available in the province like land, water, etc, but also calls for a consistent economic growth of over 3 per cent so as to maintain healthy living standards.

The rural-urban divide in Punjab is the narrowest compared to the other provinces. Rural Punjab, especially, central Punjab is very prosperous due to its links with industry, the formal economy, and with urban centres. It is also the main cotton growing area in Punjab.

Punjab has five major urban centres with a population of over one million - Lahore, Rawalpindi, Faisalabad, Multan and Gujranwala. These cities account for 48 per cent of the urban population. Nearly 21 per cent of the provincial population is concentrated in the Lahore-Faisalabad-Gujranwala belt, which is also the industrial hub of Pakistan

Lahore is the biggest industrial area in Pakistan, after Karachi. Lahore is also the most densely populated district in Punjab with 3,566 persons per sq km. There are many industrial units in the district that engage in cotton, woollen and silk clothes, carpets and rugs, leather and rubber foot wears, wearing apparel, pharmaceutical goods, soaps, iron and steel products, fabricated product, agriculture machinery, printing and publishing, etc.

The Faisalabad district, known as the heart of agriculture in Punjab, grows cotton, wheat, sugarcane, maize, rice and vegetables. Gujranwala is a prominent district in rice production. There are large industrial units for chemicals, food products, textiles and the engineering industry.

The ethnic composition of the province reveals that 75 per cent of the population are Punjabis, dominating both the urban and rural centres. The other major ethnic groups are the Seraikis making up for 17 per cent of the population. Pushtos comprise 1.2 per cent, while Balochis and Sindhis are a minority.

Though Punjab is bereft of ethnic clashes, sectarian clashes are evident. Lately, the Seraiki group has started displaying an anti-Punjabi stance in their rhetoric. The Seraiki belt in the south of Punjab, which includes the districts of Bahawalpur, Multan and Dera Ghazi Khan, is distinct from the rest of Punjab. There is widespread poverty due to poor irrigation and large landholdings. The Seraiki people from this part are the largest migrants into Karachi working as unskilled labourers.

The Seraiki belt faces discrimination at the hands of other parts of Punjab. Numerous settlers from the north have taken Seraiki lands and resources and are also in the government administration. Moreover, the army has also been given a large share of state land in these regions. Compounding this issue is the problem of access to resources and land continues to exist. There are grievances of insufficient water for irrigation.

This particular ethnic group has been feeling the brunt of injustice over many years. It has no representation in the Federal service or autonomous bodies of the Army. The growing sense of persecution has led the Seraikis to demand

Table 7.1: Punjab's Ethnic Composition

(% share)

	Punjabi	Urdu	Sindhi	Pushto	Balochi	Seraiki	Others
Rural	73.6	2.0	0.2	0.9	0.9	21.4	1.0
Urban	78.7	10.1	0.1	1.8	0.1	8.4	0.8
Total	75.2	4.5	0.1	1.2	0.7	17.4	0.9

social, cultural, political, economic and constitutional rights from Pakistan. They believe that unless they get full recognition as a fifth federating unit with the formation of the Seraiki Province, their grievances cannot be redressed, just like the Baloch of Balochistan, the Sindhis of Sindh, the Pashtuns of NWFP and the Punjabis of Punjab. However, Punjab does not recognise Seraiki as a distinct language, but has included it only as a dialect of Punjabi.

Punjab is a youthful province with 62 per cent of its population below the age group of 25. Of the 44.6 million people in this group, nearly half fall in the below-10 years category. However, of the 27 million people forming the workforce, 2 million are unemployed. Moreover, hardly 44 per cent of the working population is literate.

Economy

Agriculture is the backbone of Punjab's economy, and plays a leading role in agricultural production in the country. It contributes about 68 per cent to annual foodgrain production. Cotton, wheat and rice are important crops that contribute substantially to the provincial exchequer.

About 12 million hectares of land is cultivated in the province, accounting for over 56 per cent of the total cultivated area in the country. It has one of the best irrigation networks in the country comprising 14 major barrages with a total offtake canal capacity of 1.2 lakh cusecs of irrigation supplies and another 1.1 lakh cusecs capacity of inter-river links. The irrigation network runs over 23,000 miles. There are about 21 main canals irrigating 12.8 million hectares of land. Incidentally, 75 per cent of the total irrigated area in Pakistan lies in this province.

The sheer size of the irrigation system in the province points to its importance and the need to secure its water availability. The province receives water from both the major reservoirs, Tarbela and Mangla. Besides, the province has 31 small dams that provide irrigation facilities to about 36,000 acres of land.

Till the 1960s, Punjab had a highly agrarian economy with a contribution of 50 per cent to the provincial GDP. Having attained self-sufficiency in agriculture, the focus shifted to developing the industrial sector. Growth centres began to emerge and emphasis was laid on setting up of small-scale industries. Punjab saw a drastic transformation to its economy, enabling development of industrial zones built on solid agricultural foundation.

% Share to total GDP

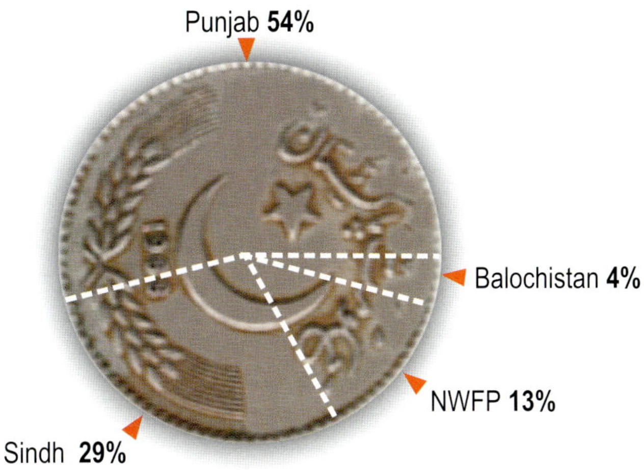

Though Karachi is the industrial hub of Pakistan, it has a concentration of large manufacturing units in petroleum, chemicals and heavy engineering unlike Punjab. Except in textiles and leather, Punjab has more units in all other categories of industry. It has approximately 39,000 small and cottage industrial units and about 6355 units for processing of agriculture raw materials like food and feed.

In fact, the most developed regions in Punjab are located around the rivers flowing in the province. Of the 34 districts, 8 districts are highly developed, 16 are in the middle development category and 10 in the low development category.

Punjab has 10.5 million households out of the 19.2 million in Pakistan with an average size of 6.9 persons per household. This province has the highest concentration of *pucca* houses – 62 per cent of total households in the province – as compared with the national average of 55 per cent. However, despite the towering economic indicators, the social indicators are quite dismal in comparison with the country.

Only a little over 25 per cent of housing units in Punjab has access to tap water. Only 17.7 per cent of the housing units have gas connections as against the national average of 20 per cent. Only over 26 per cent of the housing units have a separate latrine. Thus basic amenities are relatively poor in Punjab. However, Punjab comprises of the highest number of households electrified. Punjab also has the highest infant mortality rate in the country with 96 deaths per thousand live births. This is social poverty amidst economic prosperity.

However, the situation in recent times is very encouraging. The focus of the provincial government has been tilting towards social sector development such as education, health, employment and sanitation. There is a growing sense of urgency to provide people, with a secure and better quality of life.

Education has been on top priority for the present Punjab government. The literacy rate in the province is around 47.4 per cent, higher than the national average of 45 per cent. The literacy levels despite being the highest in the country have not been uniform within the province. There is a wide disparity between the literacy levels among districts. The highest literacy ratio is that of Rawalpindi with 70 per cent while the lowest levels of 20.7 per cent is in Rajanpur in DG Khan division.

Distribution of Illiterate Youth

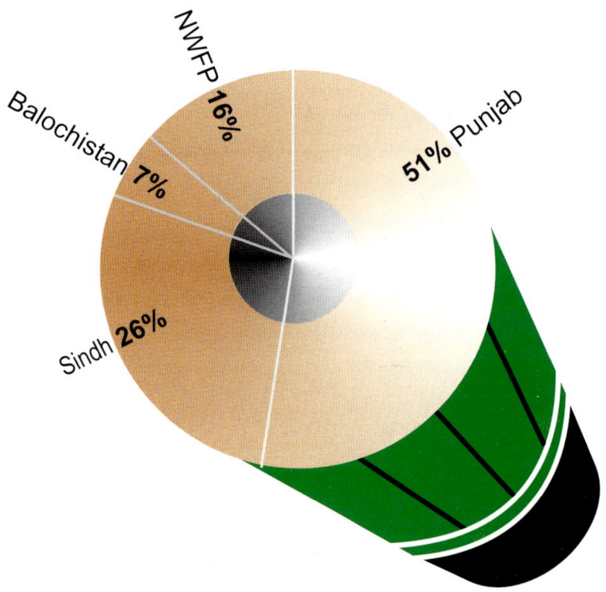

It is interesting to note that most of the districts with low literacy levels in the province are located in the southern parts of Punjab, which incidentally is the base for many terrorist organisations. While most of the terrorist outfits are based in Punjab, some of them are located in the southern and central parts of the province. The Jaish-e-Mohammed is based in Bahawalpur and sectarian outfit Lashkar-e-Jhangvi has its headquarters in Jhang. Co-incidentally, these areas have the lowest literacy levels as well. This is ominous as majority of the country's uneducated youth are in Punjab.

Agriculture

Agriculture continues to play a crucial role in Punjab's economy, which extends to influence the overall economy of Pakistan. A substantial 42 per cent of Punjab's population is directly engaged in agriculture and allied fields.

A peculiar aspect observed in Punjab is that the irrigated area far exceeds the total cultivated area. This implies that there exists irrigated land that cannot be cultivated due to its degeneration from salinity and waterlogging. Punjab is known for its highly mechanised agriculture. It is also the highest user of tractors and fertilisers in the country. Thanks to modern agricultural practices, Punjab has retained its supremacy.

Punjab produces over 78 per cent of the country's total wheat, 85 per cent of cotton, 48 per cent of rice and 78 per cent of pulses. Its contribution to fruits and vegetable production is well over 60 per cent. This clearly reveals the extent to which Punjab's agrarian economy contributes to Pakistan's food security. A significant portion of food grains, fruits and vegetables are supplied to various parts of the country. NWFP runs its flourmills from the wheat procured from Punjab.

The relationship between agricultural and industrial production is most visible in Punjab province. The major cotton producing zones are the southern and central parts of Punjab, and as a result most textile industries are concentrated in this region. Similarly, a significant section of sugar industries are located in districts of Faisalabad, Sargodha, Jhang, Bahawalpur and RY Khan, where sugarcane is cultivated.

Punjab produces the high quality *'Basmati'* rice that is largely exported. Sindh is also a major contributor to rice production, but its quality known as *Irri* has a lower value. In 2002-03, the unit value of Basmati rice was $505 per tonne, while that of Irri was $176 per tonne. This clearly reflects Punjab's high standing as an export earner.

Punjab's significance to Pakistan as a major foreign exchange earner can be gauged from the fact that it contributes 85 per cent to the country's cotton production. Cotton and related exports earns about 60 per cent of foreign earnings for Pakistan. Apart, from cotton, rice is the other major export item, which is also a high-value produce in Punjab.

The rich agricultural districts are located in central and eastern Punjab. Faisalabad district is known as the heart of agriculture with several important crops like cotton, wheat, sugarcane, maize, rice and vegetables grown here while Gujranwala district is prominent for its rice production.

It is not the technology and the abundant resources alone that have propelled the agricultural sector in Punjab, but also the government's policy of promoting agriculture and related sectors.

Water Resources in Punjab

All the major rivers in Pakistan – Indus, Jhelum, Chenab, Ravi and Sutlej – flow through this province. The Punjab irrigation network comprises of 14 major barrages with a total off-take canal capacity of 1.2 lakh cusecs of irrigation supplies and another 1.1 lakh cusecs capacity of inter-river links. The irrigation network runs over 23,000 miles. There are about 21 main canals irrigating 12.8 million hectares of land.

The province receives water from both the major reservoirs in the country – Tarbela and Mangla. Punjab reserves complete rights over the Mangla reservoir built to compensate for the rivers lost to India under the Indus Waters Treaty of 1960. It draws water from this reserve during kharif season, and takes water from Tarbela, through the Chashma-Jhelum Link Canal and Taunsa Barrage, for its rabi crop.

Shortage in irrigation water supply has affected Punjab as well. In 2001-02, the province suffered water shortage to the extent of 34 per cent. In 2002-03, however, due to improved availability, water shortages mitigated to 18 per cent.

The problems of salinity and waterlogging afflict Punjab too, though with lower intensity than Sindh. About 1.7 million hectares of land in Punjab is underlain by saline groundwater. The canal irrigation system in Punjab renders 100,000 acres of land unproductive every year through water logging and salinity.

Due to drought conditions in recent years, around 6,000 villages in Attock, Jhang, Chakwal, Dera Ghazi Khan and Rajanpur districts of Punjab had to be declared calamity-hit in mid-2002. In addition, the rain fed regions namely Potohar belt, Mianwali and southern districts of Punjab continue to be drought-affected.

Punjab has been undertaking projects to develop and integrate its irrigation system for securing water availability. A scheme to divert the Chenab to join it with the Ravi and Sutlej is on the anvil. To improve the water conditions in rain fed areas, the government intends to build three small dams in Potohar, DG Khan and Cholistan areas in 2004. Plans are also afoot to build 60 mini dams, 100 link mini dams and 200 village reservoirs in the Potohar region.

The provincial government has also decided to launch a Rs.20 billion irrigation system rehabilitation project to overcome system losses, estimated at around 40 to 50 per cent. The project, proposed to begin in the current fiscal (2003-04) with an initial allocation of Rs.500 million, will be completed by 2007-08. It will cover the irrigation systems in Lahore, Bahawalpur, Faisalabad, Sargodha, Multan and Dera Ghazi Khan.

Minerals

Punjab has a low profile in Pakistan's mineral map. Unlike Balochistan and Sindh, Punjab cannot boast of any major mineral resources. The province has limited energy resources like oil, gas and coal.

Punjab contributes hardly seven per cent to total gas production, 30 per cent to oil and 15 per cent of coal production. The province has hardly 2 per cent of mineable coal reserves in the province.

Punjab nevertheless is the largest consumer of these resources in the country, owing to the large population it houses. Punjab accounts for over 56 per cent of petroleum products consumed in the country. The province also has over 50 per cent of Pakistan's total gas consumers.

Punjab is a net importer of energy resources.

Industry

The agriculturally advanced province of Punjab witnessed the emergence of industrial centres only during 1960s. This could be attributed to the success of the green revolution, which inspired the rich landlords to diversify into the industrial sector.

The advantage of easy accessibility to raw materials and the commercial markets were prevalent in certain areas. Development of infrastructure along with the presence of skilled labour fuelled the expansion and development of the industrial sectors. By the year 2000, Punjab had over sixty thousand industrial units with industrial zones in nearly every administrative division.

Cottage and small-scale industries play a very important role in the province, as they are mainstay of the province's industrial sector. Punjab founded its own provincial small industries corporation (PSIC) in 1972. The early small industrial estates were established in Gujranwala, Sialkot and Gujrat for light engineering, sports and surgical goods, leather and other export oriented goods.

When Pakistan entered the world carpet market during 1973-80, even remote districts like DG Khan, Layyah and Ahmedpur came into prominence. Following the success of these industries, additional industrial estates were set up in the early 1980's in Chakwal, Jhelum, Gujjar Khan, Sargodha, Sahiwal and Faisalabad. By the late 1990's, small industries catering to furniture and wood works were set up in Khanewal, Taxila and Kasur.

The small-scale industry in Punjab is the largest in the country, and is highly diversified ranging from manufacturing textiles, sports goods to agricultural products. The Faisalabad district houses the maximum number of industries and is primarily a textile zone.

In conclusion, though Punjab is rich in agricultural resources, it depends on other provinces for its industrial and service sector development. Punjab has no energy security of its own, and banks on the other smaller provinces to fuel its industry. This is a crucial dependence that Punjab has built on the other provinces.

Small groups, while expressing dissent over Punjab's dominance have successfully exploited Punjab's energy dependence. Targeting gas supply pipelines to Punjab therefore is commonplace. Without energy resources, Punjab would be relegated to being merely a primary agriculture province, with no value addition. Unless, Punjab steps up its sources of energy, which is unlikely given the poor energy resources, it will continue to remain subservient to the smaller ones.

Table7.2: Industrial Units in Punjab (1999-2000)

Division	Number of Industrial Units
Bhawalpur	1,677
DG Khan	2,671
Faisalabad	15,084
Gujranwala	13,546
Lahore	13,251
Multan	7,102
Rawalpindi	4,216
Sargodha	2,528
The Punjab	60,075

However, the province has always remained under the tutelage of the federal government and is therefore rather unmindful of its energy deficiency. Moreover, army patronage has benefited the province the most.

Relations with the Centre

Punjab shares a symbiotic relationship with the centre. It is the most powerful province in the country, propped up by the federal government. Due to its immense size in all respects, it has a crucial role in the decision-making processes of the country. It has the added benefit of being home to the army and the federal government of Pakistan.

A large portion, about 52 per cent of the federal bureaucracy, comprises Punjabis. This is also the case in the army, where the Punjabis hold about 60.31 per cent of the top posts. Most policies therefore have favoured Punjab.

Punjab and the centre are interdependent - politically, economically and financially. This is what reinforces their relationship.

Population as a basis for allocation of financial resources has provided Punjab the much-needed leverage to undertake economic development. The province has been recipient of the highest allocation, on the strength of its sheer size.

Punjab finances 18 per cent of its own expenditures, leaving a large 82 per cent to be funded through external sources. The transfers from the divisible pool by the National Finance Commission make a significant impact on the province's finances. The province moreover does not much enjoy the benefit of direct transfers in the form of royalty, for there is very limited production of mineral resources in the province.

Punjab is therefore the only province that supports the population criteria for allocation of financial resources by the federal government. Perhaps, this could be one of the factors that has dissuaded the province from undertaking extensive population control measures.

Table 7.3: Tax Revenues from Punjab

Taxes Collected		Share Paid	
Rs.billion	% Share	Rs.billion	% Share
192.204	21.55	194.181	58.09

Source: Business Recorder, Sept 5, 2003 Sindh's Case for a better NFC deal: Mohamed Anwar and Raza Haroon

Punjab is the second largest contributor to the national exchequer after Sindh, with a share of around 23 per cent. However, its receipts are incommensurate. While taxes collected from the Punjab make up 22 per cent of the total taxes collected, the share paid to it by the federal government is about 58 per cent of the total tax collection.

Punjab is the only province that manages to regularly generate a surplus budget. In the year 2003-04, it is expected to have an excess of Rs.22 billion in its coffers. The Punjab budget reflects strong fiscal management. Fiscal 2003-04 has been exceptionally good for the province as it hopes to redeem a major part of its debt due to the Centre.

Punjab is the biggest beneficiary of the ultimate benefactor in Pakistan - the central government and the army. It has had the least worries in fiscal management of the province. Funds flow has been assured. Federal government-sponsored projects have mainly benefited Punjab. Being an agrarian economy, due care was taken to reinforce its irrigation and water supply network. Mechanisation of agriculture was foremost undertaken in Punjab. During the 1970s, policies were promoted to enable industrialisation in the province. Energy supplies were assured through a well-networked gas, oil and electricity distribution system. Such promotion of a single province, at the cost of other provinces, brought not only a revolutionary change within Punjab, but also created a formidable image in the eyes of the other provinces.

It is in the interest of the federal government to keep the provinces united for the sake of Punjab's prosperity. Punjab's dependence on the other provinces is crucial for its survival, as vital inputs from the smaller provinces sustain Punjab - gas from Balochistan, coal and port access from Sindh, water from NWFP and Kashmir (Pakistan) and funds from the central government. All the smaller provinces have had justifiable grouses against Punjab.

Political Management

The ruling class of Pakistan mainly consists of Punjabis, irrespective of whether it was a democratic government or the army ruling the country. In 1997, during Nawaz Sharief's rule, most of the people holding key positions were from Punjab, especially central Punjab. Rather than having a national representation, the cabinet gave the impression of being more of a central Punjab government. Nawaz Sharief's brother, Shahbaz Sharief was the then Chief Minister of Punjab.

The most popular political party in Punjab was the Pakistan Muslim League (PML) headed by Nawaz Sharief and promoted by Zia-ul-H aq. Mian Nawaz Sharief ruled Punjab from 1985 to 1990 and later moved on to become the Prime Minister of the country for two terms. Even during Benazir Bhutto's rule in Pakistan from 1993-96, the PML (N) ruled Punjab. The PML (N) is known to be a pro-military party. However, the party split into several factions, and during General Musharraf's rule, Nawaz Sharief was forced into exile. This somewhat eroded the credibility of the party, and Musharraf decided to promote the other PML factions to form the government. He created conditions for the win of PML (Quaid-e-Azam) faction, who are today the ruling party in Punjab as well as the federal government.

Provincial Share in Federal Bureaucracy

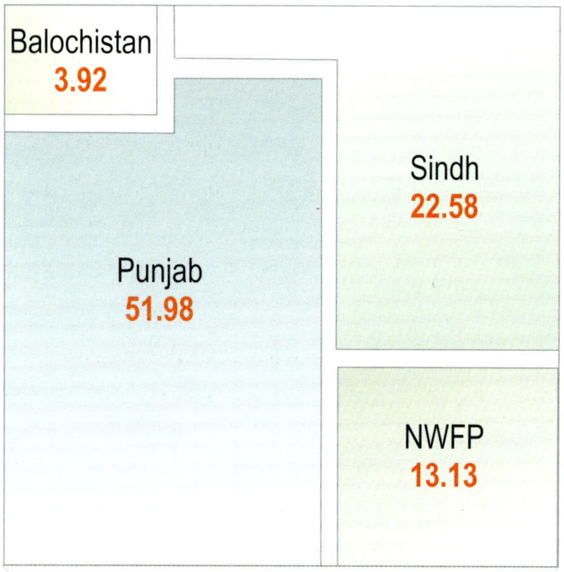

In most instances, the party that ruled at the centre has governed Punjab. This was especially true in the case of the Punjab-based parties – whenever the PML (N) ruled at the centre, they also governed Punjab. Pakistan has had a long history of military domination, and military rule is always associated with increased Punjabi domination. Military generals are known to own several acres of land in Punjab and Sindh. Recently, the revenue board of Punjab government revealed that 112 military officers, including General Musharraf, were allotted agricultural land at nominal rates in the Cholistan area of southern Punjab. This prompted the government to undertake the Thal canal project, much to the consternation of Sindh, to irrigate the areas owned by military personnel. Thus, army rule has helped prosper and develop Punjab to a large extent. The military also owns several industrial assets in Punjab.

Punjab dominates the bureaucracy too. With the federal government at the helm of appointing top bureaucrats, Punjabis get appointed to top positions in other provinces as well, indirectly promoting Punjabi interests. Moreover, Punjabis appointed abroad as envoys are also known to promote their province's interest.

Though Punjab is dominant in all respects – demographically, economically, and even linguistically – it is difficult to establish this argument politically. Apart from Nawaz Sharief, all leaders in the country since 1971 have been non-Punjabis. Zulfikar Ali Bhutto from Sindh, Zia-ul-Haq an East Pakistan migrant, Benazir Bhutto, Ghulam Mustafa Jatoi and Junejo were Sindhis, General Pervez Musharraf a mohajir and the present Mir Zafarullah Khan Jamali a Baloch. Both pre-partition military rulers, Yahya Khan and Ayub Khan, were Pathans.

Several regional political parties from Sindh, Balochistan and NWFP have been seeking independence from a Punjab-dominated Pakistan. Though these leaders stress the need for a unified Pakistan, they are unwilling to accept a Pakistan dominated by a single ethnic group. In a meeting held in Islamabad, on February 22, 2004, under the aegis of PONM (Pakistan Oppressed Nations Movement), there was a distinct anti-Punjab and anti-military sentiment running among the leaders. There was a clear demand for autonomy and independence from Punjab. The leaders on stage included Ataullah Mengal, Baloch leader and convener of PONM, Mahmood Khan Achakzai President of Paktoonkhwa Milli Awami Party, leaders of JSQM. Slogans of "Sindhudesh zindabad, Balochistan zindabad, Pakhtoonkwah zindabad and Seraikistan zindabad" were raised. This was clearly indicative of their disenchantment towards Punjab. These very leaders, once acquiesced to be with Pakistan, are now disappointed.

Prospects

Growth

Punjab's economy, though agrarian and not as well diversified as Sindh's, will remain crucial to Pakistan's food security. By present thinking, Punjab has excellent prospects for economic growth. The ruling government of Punjab, under Pervez Elahi, is focussing towards developing a strong infrastructure, emphasising on power and water resources. If it succeeds in setting up a strong infrastructure base, Punjab will definitely witness an economic upsurge.

Punjab's economic success also depends on maintaining good relations with the other provinces. Punjab cannot have an isolated existence. It is highly dependent on the other provinces for its energy and water supply, mineral resources and access to international markets. Without these life-sustaining inputs, it would be difficult for Punjab to even exist.

If relations with the other provinces improve, and Punjab manages to mellow its condescending stance, Punjab's economy will greatly benefit. This would have an overall beneficial impact on Pakistan's economy as well in light of the contribution made by this single province. Also, a major part of the population will find productive jobs followed by better living conditions and well-being.

However, if Pakistan splits, it would have a grave impact on Punjab's economy. If Sindh and Balochistan secede, Punjab will be left landlocked and deprived of energy resources. If NWFP also secedes, water flows into Punjab will get impacted, affecting the province's massive population. The internal turmoil thus created, in conjunction with the *jihadi* groups, can lead the province towards becoming a terror base.

An area of concern for Punjab is however its social sector development. Since the province is home to the largest part of Pakistan's population, it is imperative for Punjab to provide a strong social base – in terms of educational and health facilities – that resists *jihadi* culture.

God

Punjab is the biggest centre for *jihad* in Pakistan with more than 50 per cent of *jihadis* coming from this province. So far, over 12,000 have sacrificed for the sake of *jihad* from Punjab, of which 4,000 died in the Afghan *jihad* and 8,000 in Kashmir.

There are over 5,500 religious seminaries in the province. Of these, 3,000 belong to the Deobandi school of thought, 1,500 are Barelvis, 800 are Ahle Hadis and 120 are Shia seminaries. Extremist religious parties also have a presence in the province. Jamaat-e-Islami has 100 seminaries in the province.

Punjab is the largest centre for *jihadi* and extremist recruitments. The sectarian group, Sipah-e-Sahaba has 16 offices all over the province, out of 28 in the entire country. The Lashkar-e-Taiba has 29 centres for recruitment, Jaish-e-Mohammad has nine centres and other Kashmir-based *jihadi* groups, excluding the LeT and Hizbul Mujahideen, have 14 centres all over Punjab. Most recruits come from the underdeveloped regions of Multan, Bahawalpur and DG Khan districts of the province.

More than ideology, it is heroism that attracts the youth of Punjab to join *jihad*. Moreover, for the poor, the social security

Future Scenarios

The Dawn

SCENARIO **1**

In this scenario, Pak experiences a new dawn of economic progress and reconciliation between provinces. Its thoroughgoing on the economic front promotes sustained growth and helps meet global challenges. The US continues to favour Pakistan thus facilitating inflow of aid. The army decides to move out of political governance, and allow the establishment of democracy. The democratic government embarks upon a reorganisation of provinces, creating many more provinces so as to dilute the strong ethnic identity of the provinces. It also prunes its own stronghold on the provinces thus bestowing autonomy. On another front, it contains *jihadi* activities, though it is unable to completely wipe out the menace. Internal stability brings investments, leading to development and Pakistan becoming an attractive destination for foreign investment. Relations with neighbouring countries also improve, who also realise the benefits of maintaining good relations with Pakistan.

SIGNPOSTS

- Sound economic policies
- Continuation of foreign aid
- Infusion of investments
- Resolution of Punjab-Sindh water conflict to mutual satisfaction
- Reorganisation of provinces thus leading to a fair distribution of fiscal resources and royalty
- Return of democracy
- Containment of *jihadi* forces
- Success in operations in FATA, making inroads into the region
- Normal relations with India, Afghanistan and Iran
- Balanced relations with US and China
- Stability in Afghanistan

SCENARIO 2

In this scenario, there is emphasis on economic progress wherever feasible with complete disregard for political consequences. Grievances of provinces go un-addressed, while the federal government continues to promote the interests of the army and the elite. The army remains the *de facto* ruler of Pakistan. Development takes place in certain pockets of the country, thus leading to sharp regional disparities. These differences are glaringly visible in Sindh. Punjab continues to enjoy overall benefits, with its supply-lines taken care of by the governing elite. As a result, differences between Sindh and Punjab aggravate, though not reaching a stage of a rebellion. Internal instability provides a boost to *jihadi* activities, who spread their tentacles all across the country. The religious and modern political parties continue to remain in discord. The army continues to maintain a conflict-relationship with India to divert attention from internal political instability, and retain its stranglehold.

SIGNPOSTS

- Development of Punjab, Gwadar, pockets of Sindh and NWFP
- Sharp regional disparities
- Foreign aid continues to come in
- Good exports and remittances inflow
- Development of mineral and electricity sector
- Construction of Kalabagh dam
- Serious tensions between Punjab and Sindh over water distribution
- Army's domination with a democratic facade
- Increasing conflict between *jihadis* and modernists
- Increase in separatist agitations
- Corruption at its peak
- Instability but no explosion in Afghanistan
- Conflict-relations with India.

Dastak

SCENARIO 3

In this scenario, the domination by the army-based institutions ensures unity on the surface, but ring a warning bell for ensuing problems. Political unity is superficially maintained under the command of the army, but in-fighting among them increases. This leaves the polity of Pakistan fractured, and army control prevails. However, the economic front is also suffering due to political preoccupation. The volatile internal situation deters any further foreign investments into the country, and public investments are also cut down as funds are diverted for other non-development purposes. This results in increasing unemployment and poverty levels. Extremist religious groups who find propitious circumstances to promote *jihadi* culture. Madrassas crop up, *jihadi* forces increase. While *jihadis* are flourishing, the provinces' grievances are violently suppressed.

SIGNPOSTS

- Economic growth suffering due to preoccupation with political developments
- Low investment levels
- Increase in unemployment and poverty levels
- Army rule continues
- Punjab's domination maintained
- Construction of Thal canal to the consternation of Sindh
- Debate continues, but no action on Kalabagh dam construction
- Substantial increase in water disputes
- Heavy crackdown on separatist agitations
- Heavy crackdown in FATA and Balochistan, along with entry of army in these regions
- Increase in strength of *jihadi* groups but controlled by the army
- Tensions between religious parties and modernists continue
- Tensions with all neighbours
- Heavy US role

Jang

SCENARIO 4

In this scenario, there is severe conflict among the provinces leading to a break-up of the country. Pakistan proves to be a failed state, with provinces trying to secede. Economy is on the downslide. Punjab is a victim of the smaller provinces wrath and its supply lines are choked. The *jihadis* take the opportunity to control the state, which is made possible by a faction within the army. A series of coups finally installs a leader who rules in obedience to religious leaders and change the course of national policies. Sindh, Balochistan and NWFP decide to break away from Punjabi domination, and decide to secede on ethnic lines. NWFP and Balochistan decide to merge with their respective ethnic factions, while Sindh undergoes a major turmoil with mohajirs and Sindhis vying for control of the province. Amidst internal fights, international powers also make Pakistan their battlefield to gain control over the region.

SIGNPOSTS

- Unemployment, poverty is rampant
- Foreign aid flows dry up
- Supply lines to Punjab are sabotaged, thus choking its economy
- Increase in *jihadi* activities
- Series of army coups
- Capture of Pakistani state by *jihadis* in partnership with a section of the army
- Sindh, Balochistan and NWFP seek separation
- Demand for reorganisation of Pakhtoonistan from parts of Afghanistan and Pakistan
- Baloch unity is forged between the ethnic groups in Iran, Afghanistan and Pakistan
- Massive inflow of refugees into India and Iran
- Direct US intervention
- Intense US-China cooperation followed by intense conflict

References

Ahmad, Manzoor and Ghaus, Khalida, 1999, *Pakistan, Prospects and Perspectives*, Karachi: Royal Book Company

Ahmed, Feroz, 2000, *Ethnicity and Politics in Pakistan*, Karachi: Oxford University Press

Economic Adviser's Wing, Ministry of Finance, http://www.finance.gov.pk, 2000-2001, 2001-2002, 2002-2003, *Economic Survey of Pakistan*, Islamabad: Government of Pakistan

Ewart, J.M, 2000, *Story of the North West Frontier Province*, Lahore: Sang-e-Meel Publications

Federal Bureau of Statistics of Pakistan, http://www.statpak.gov.pk, *Pakistan Statistical Yearbook 2003, Labour Force Survey 2001-02*

Ghauri, Iqbal Javed (editor), 1998, *Pakistan Chronology 1947-1997*, Islamabad: Government of Pakistan

Hasan, Parvez, 1998, *Pakistan's Economy at the Crossroads*, Karachi: Oxford University Press

Hussain, Ishrat, 2002, *Pakistan The Economy of an Elitist State*, Karachi: Oxford University Press

Hydrocarbon Development Institute of Pakistan, Ministry of Petroleum and Natural Resources, January 2003, *Pakistan Energy Yearbook, 2002*, Islamabad: Government of Pakistan

Khan, M.H (editor), 2001, *The Pakistan Budgets 2001-2002*, Karachi: Royal Book Company

Kundi, Mansoor Akbar, 1994, *Balochistan A Socio-Cultural and Political Analysis*, Quetta: Qasim Printers

Mahbub ul Haq Human Development Centre, 1998, 1999, 2001, 2002, *Human Development in South Asia*, Karachi: Oxford University Press

Shariff, K.M. (editor), 2001, *Pakistan Almanac 2000-2001*, Karachi, Royal Book Company

Smoke, Paul and Kim, Yun-Hwan (editors), *Intergovernmental Fiscal Transfers in Asia: Current Practice and Challenges for the Future, Chapter 6 Pakistan by Ahmad, Nuzhat and Wasti, Syed Ashraf*, Asian Development Bank

Social Policy and Development Centre, 2001, *Social Development in Pakistan (Annual Review 2000)*, Karachi: Oxford University Press

State Bank of Pakistan, Ministry of Finance, Government of Pakistan, http://www.sbp.org.pk

Waslekar, Sundeep, et al, 2002, *Future of Pakistan*, Mumbai: International Centre for Peace Initiatives

Zaidi, Akbar S., 2000, *Issues in Pakistan's Economy*, Karachi: Oxford University Press

Zaidi, Akbar S. (editor), 1992, *Regional Imbalances & The National Question in Pakistan*, Karachi: Vanguard Books (Pvt) Ltd.

Zaidi, Akbar S. (editor), 2003, *Continuity and Change: Socio-Political and Institutional Dynamics in Pakistan*, Karachi: City Press

Directorate of Agriculture, Balochistan, http://www.agricbal.sdnpk.org

Government of Punjab website, http://www.punjab.gov.pk, *Punjab Statistics*

Government of Sindh website, http://www.sindh.gov.pk, *Sindh at a Glance*

Population Association of Pakistan, http://www.pap.org.pk

Sindh Bureau of Statistics, http://www.sbos.sdnpk.org,

NWFP Bureau of Statistics, http://www/nwfpbos.sdnpk.org

Balochistan Bureau of Statistics, http://www.bdd.sdnpk.org

Newspapers and Magazines

Ausaf, Akhbar-e-Jehan, Balochistan Post, Business Recorder

Daily Times, Dawn, Friday Times, Herald, Ibrat, Jang, Jasarat

Kawish, Nation, Nawa-i-Waqt, News International

Pakistan and Gulf Economist, Takbeer

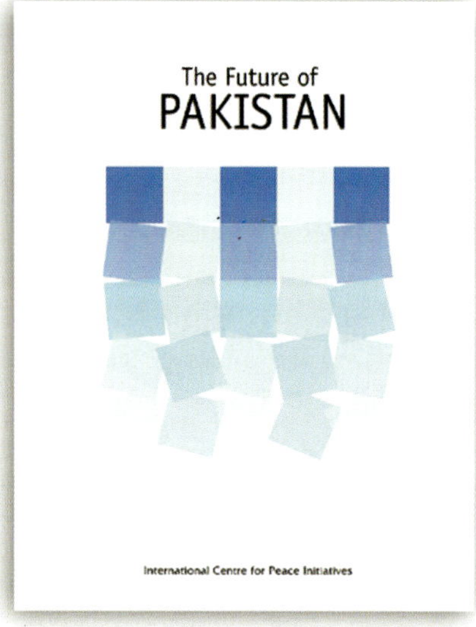

The Future of Pakistan

India Rs. 1,050
Abroad US$ 45

ISBN 81-88262-00-5

The report looks at Pakistan in view of its central role in the war in Afghanistan. General Pervez Musharraf has supported the US led coalition and vowed to free Pakistan of sectarianism and terrorism. Can he succeed? How long will he survive in the hot seat in Rawalpindi? What will be the policies of his successor? Will orthodox religious forces seize control of the Pakistani state, and if so when? How will Pakistan's economy perform in the next ten years? Will there be adequate food and water? Will Sindh and Baluchistan try to separate from Pakistan? Will there be a war between India and Pakistan? What will be the cause of the next major India-Pakistan war, since it will not be over Kashmir? Will nuclear weapons be used? The report answers the above questions and more, using scientific methods of strategic foresight. Since its publication in May 2002, many of the forecasts made in the report have already come true.

"It is almost vital for decision makers and opinion shapers in India particularly, and the international community generally, to seriously look at this very readable study packed with empirical data to support the analysis."

- **Jasjit Singh, in The Indian Express, October 2, 2002**

"I completely agree with the way you have described tensions in the military and the uncertainties about General Musharraf's ability to control...... a really, really fabulous report."

- **Jessica Stern, Kennedy School of Government, Harvard University**

Rethinking India's Future: Prosperity of the Periphery

India Rs. 625
Abroad US$ 25

ISBN 81-88262-02-1

The report outlines India's development model that has created three economies- business class, bike and bullock cart economy. Will this division of the Indian economy cause a division of the Indian mind, or will unity of the Indian mind lead to the integration and transformation of the Indian economy? What does the future hold for India? Three scenarios have been put forward: Breakdown, Break-up and Breakthrough. What will be the appropriate strategies to make the best scenario possible? Will India manage to place herself in a virtuous cycle of prosperity and peace? This report provides insightful and innovate answers to these questions. It is essential reading for anyone who is interested in India's future.

"...Very informative and gives insights into the role of agro-industrial revolution for the development of India, especially the rural people."

- Bhairon Singh Shekhawat, Vice President of India

"...Valuable material on India's future. We are all pushing for a breakthrough."

- Fidel Ramos, former President of the Philippines

"The Group analysed vast quantities of data and interviewed a large number of individuals involved in public life to track emerging trends, analyse their consequences and offer policy guidelines to shape a brighter future for the nation..... What the report has done, in substance, is to implore the beneficiaries of the business class economy to emerge from their smug world of make believe before the rising discontent in 98 per cent of India's population sees them running helter-skelter for cover."

- Dileep Padgaonkar, in The Sunday Times, December 1, 2002

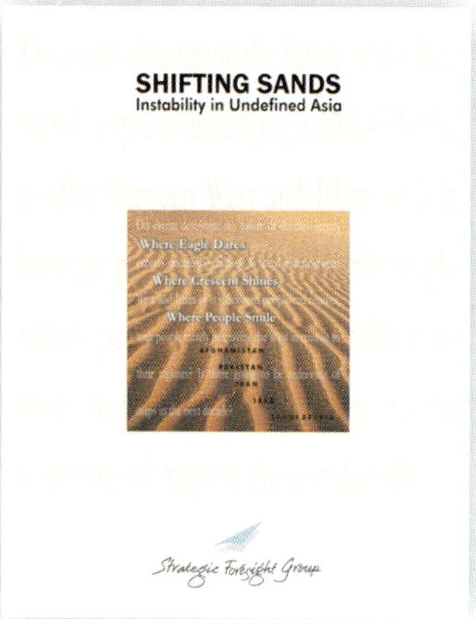

Shifting Sands: Instability in Undefined Asia

India Rs. 1350
Abroad US$ 60

ISBN 81-88262-03-X

The report addresses tensions between the impact of events and underlying structural realities in Undefined Asia consisting of Pakistan, Afghanistan, Iran, Iraq and Saudi Arabia. Though undefined as it is outside any established institutional arrangements or group of nations, it is interlinked by oil, terrorism, and strategic concerns of big powers.

As the US military involvement in Afghanistan and Iraq creates a spell of uncertainty many questions are bound to come to surface. Will the US actions in Undefined Asia primarily determine the future of the region? Or are there internal dynamics, which render US actions superficial?

Many of the predictions made in Shifting Sands have proved to be correct within a few months of its publication. The report had predicted the withdrawal of American forces from Saudi Arabia, armed skirmishes between Afghanistan and Pakistan, rise of terrorism in Undefined Asia following the US victory in Baghdad. Many other predictions await the test of time. In order to understand what will happen in the world's largest hot spot in the first decade of the twenty first century, the report is a must read for everyone.

"In today's world it is hard to imagine any study being more timely and relevant.... I find much of your analysis and many of your conclusions very persuasive."

- *Katherine Marshall,* Counsellor to the President of the World Bank

"Excellent report, based on an original analysis methodology that draws interesting conclusions about the future of a highly destabilized and uncertain region."

- *Gareth Evans,* President, International Crisis Group

Cost of Conflict between India and Pakistan

India Rs. 625
Abroad US$ 30

ISBN 81-88262-04-8

The report presents comprehensive estimates of past, present and future costs of conflict between India and Pakistan. It goes beyond conventional measures of costs such as defence expenditure and opportunity cost of trade to cover varied parameters such as discounting of GDP growth rate, size of terror economy, negative transformation of institutions, politicide, diplomatic losses, educational costs, value deficit, and most importantly, human costs. It is a rare report prepared with research input from both India and Pakistan.

"The publication is highly relevant in this time and age. I congratulate the SFG for the high quality of research and analysis that has gone into the publication of the book and the intelligent use of reader-friendly graphics to illustrate various points. I am sure that the publication will prove to be of considerable value to scholars of India Pakistan relations as well as practitioners offoreignpolicy."

- Shri Yashwant Sinha, the then Minister of External Affairs, India

"This document is of exceptional quality in its comprehensive coverage and analytical strengths. It is the first time that we have such all encompassing information and analysis in one place on the implications of adversarial relationship between India and Pakistan."

- Niaz A. Naik, Pakistan's Former Foreign Secretary, Foreword

"We've known it all along the conflict with Pakistan is a lose-lose situation for both sides. But now the report of the Strategic Foresight Group titled 'Cost of Conflict between India and Pakistan ' has put a figure to it... The writing is on the wall investment in people is an investment in peace.

- Editorial, The Times of India, February 26, 2004

Notes